"As he descended from the pulpit, he was met by an aged man."

Why Delay? Frontispiece. See p. 124.

WHY DELAY?

BY

JACOB HELFFENSTEIN, D.D.

I made haste, and delayed not, to keep thy commandments.—Psalm cxix. 60.

PHILADELPHIA:
PRESBYTERIAN PUBLICATION COMMITTEE,
1334 CHESTNUT STREET.
NEW YORK: A. D. F. RANDOLPH, 770 BROADWAY.

STEREOTYPED BY WESTCOTT & THOMSON.

INVOCATION.

God of infinite mercy! in whose hands are the hearts of all men, accompany with thy blessing this humble endeavor to win souls to Thee. Engage the reader's attention, and dispose him to yield a prompt obedience to the truth, as it is here presented; and as thine is the power, thine shall be the glory, world without end. Amen.

CONTENTS.

WHY DELAY?

CHAPTER I.

TENDENCY TO DELAY—A COMMON EVIL.

THIS volume is especially intended for those who are delaying the great interest of their salvation.

Strange as it may appear, it is nevertheless true, that the subject which demands man's first and principal attention, is commonly deferred to the last. The language of the Roman Governor, when trembling under the appeals of divine truth, is the language of thousands at the present day:—"*Go thy way for this time, when I have a convenient season I will call for thee.*"

There are but few men, in a gospel land, who are not convinced of the reality and importance of religion, and who do not promise themselves that they will, at some period, give it their serious attention. As immortal and accountable beings they feel that some preparation must be made for eternity, nor would they, on any consideration, form the deliberate purpose to defer that preparation always. They mean to repent, mean to embrace Christ as their Saviour, mean to call on God for mercy, only not at present. The time is ever future, and commonly wholly indefinite. It may be in their last hour; it may be on a bed of sickness; it may be in advanced age; it may be when they become settled in life, and accumulate a certain amount of property; it may be next year or next month—only *not just now.* With the presumptive hope that death is yet remote, that the day of grace will be prolonged, and that existing difficulties will be removed or be diminished, the claims of God are deferred from one period of life to another, until probation closes, and the doom of the soul is sealed for ever.

Speak even to the child on the subject of religion, and his little bosom may be seen heaving with emotion, and his eyes filling with tears. The simple truths which you present to him, commend themselves to his understanding and conscience. The story of the cross is invested with the deepest interest; but his secret response to all the claims of a redeeming Saviour is—" not now, but—hereafter!"

Mark that young man. His pious father has just been urging him to give his attention to the one thing needful. He readily admits the importance of the subject, and finds it no easy matter to resist the appeals of parental solicitude. He means, he says, to become a Christian, but not at present. How can he now give up his gay associates; how can he abandon his worldly pleasures, and enter upon the self-denying duties connected with a life of godliness? Perhaps he has just received a letter from home. It is a most affectionate and urgent entreaty to dedicate himself to the service of Christ. Tears drop upon its pages, and a struggle takes place between conscience and inclination. He is half persuaded to yield to his convictions of duty; but he hesitates, lays the letter aside, and forms the desperate purpose to delay the great concern to some more convenient season.

See that young lady. Her Christian mother has been pleading with her to give her heart to God—to choose that good part which shall not be taken from her. "Will you not, my child, join me in my course to heaven? You have been the subject of my constant prayers and of my tenderest anxieties. Early were you dedicated to God, and ever since I have not ceased to bear you on my heart before the throne of grace. You cannot tell what joy it would afford me to find my prayers answered, and to see you seated with me at the table of our Lord—united now in Christian bonds, and in holy fellowship forever." "Dear mother," is the response, "all that you have said, is true; and I know that I ought to be a Christian, but I cannot become one now. Let me first enjoy the world. This is the time to enjoy it. It will be time enough to give my attention to religion when I become settled in life, or when overtaken by the infirmities of age; I may then need other sources of happiness than can be derived from the world."

There, too, is the man absorbed in the business and cares of earth. His devoted wife has been entreating him to become the friend of that Saviour who is the object of her warmest affections—to erect a family altar, and unite with her in training up their offspring for God and heaven. Hard indeed does he find it to resist her tears and importunity. He is convinced of his duty, but his heart still clings to the world. "Do not," he replies, "press the matter upon me now—

my mind is too much distracted, and my time too much occupied with the concerns of this world. Wait a little longer. I will join you soon."

Here is a man in vigorous health. He has just listened to an impressive sermon. His feelings have been deeply moved; he has retired from the sanctuary almost overwhelmed with the momentous theme, "Shall I or shall I not yield myself to the claims of God?" A tremendous conflict is going on within him, until it terminates in a deliberate resistance of his convictions. There are at present, he thinks, no signs of speedy death; his constitution is firm and vigorous; his health uninterrupted and his prospects bright. Why need he be in haste to make preparation for eternity?

Do you see that invalid? Mark his feeble steps, his wasting frame, his sunken eye. How rapidly he seems to be drawing near to his long home. Whatever pleas others may make for the neglect of religion, surely he can make none. If he means to attend to the subject at all, it must secure his attention without delay. But no; the convenient season has not yet come. Some Christian friend has kindly admonished him to improve the remnant of time still allotted him—to do what is to be done quickly. "What! do you think my case so alarming? I feel, indeed, somewhat enfeebled, but I hope soon to regain my former health. I shall then be more regular in my attendance at the house of God, and, I trust, shall give my serious attention to the great concern."

Turn now to that veteran in sin, bending beneath the weight of three-score years. Does he mean to be saved? Surely he does. Why then does he not at once secure an interest in the great salvation? Does he not know that his probation is drawing to a close, and that his spirit is soon to pass away to meet God in judgment? He does, he admits it all; but then he is not quite ready yet to break his grasp of earth, and fix his thoughts on heaven. God has spared him so long, that he hopes to be spared still longer. His last sickness is yet to come, and when that comes, he intends to improve his time, to call on God in prayer, and he questions not that mercy will be extended to him even in the eleventh hour.

Fix your eye on that anxious countenance. There is one in whose heart the arrows of truth have been fastened. Deep conviction has taken hold of his conscience. He feels that as a sinner he must repent or perish. His former peace has fled, and he is half persuaded to lay hold on the hope set before him in the gospel. Oh, why does he not at once cast himself into the arms of his pleading Saviour? Why does he not carry that burden of guilt to the foot of the cross, and there find pardon and life? Some hinderance yet keeps him back. He does not feel enough yet—he has not wept and prayed long enough yet. How can he go just as he is—so vile, so unworthy! He hesitates; he lingers, until the Spirit, grieved by his indecision, leaves him to wander into still greater perplexities, or to sink back to his former indifference.

CHAPTER II.

THE REAL DIFFICULTY.

WHEN we consider the general neglect of religion, we are naturally led to inquire into the *cause* of that neglect. That cause is not commonly to be found in the want of an intellectual conviction of the importance of the subject itself; for there are numbers who admit the importance of religion, who, notwithstanding, refuse practically to recognize its claims. Nor is it to be found in the peculiar circumstances in which they are placed, and which they may regard as unfavorable for giving their serious attention to the matter; for let their circumstances be ever so favorable, and they manifest the same reluctance to yield to their convictions of duty—the same disposition to put off the claims of the gospel to the future. The difficulty relates not to time or to age; for it is felt at one period of life as well as at another—in childhood, in youth, in middle-life, and even in advanced age. The real difficulty exists in THE HEART, a heart averse to all good, and prone to all evil, a heart alienated from God, and unwilling to be in subjection to his authority. "They hold fast deceit; they refuse to return." "We have loved strangers, and after them we will go." "The wicked through the pride of his countenance will not seek after God." "Ye will not come to me that ye might have life."

However much the requirements of God commend themselves to the conscience, they meet with no cordial response in the heart. The gospel requires men to be holy, but they love sin; it requires them to be humble, but they are proud; it requires them to be benevolent, but they are selfish; it requires them to seek supremely the glory of God, but they are absorbed in their own interests and pursuits; it requires implicit trust in Christ as their only Saviour, but they are prone to trust in themselves.

To all these requirements the natural heart is directly hostile, and from this arises the painful conflict which is experienced when men attempt to apply their minds to the things of religion. When the truth is brought home to their consciences, their hearts rise in opposition to it. When they feel that something must be done to secure their salvation, and they make an effort to give their thoughts to the subject, they find their way beset with difficulties. They strive, perhaps, to bring their reluctant hearts to yield, but they still retain their stubbornness, until discouraged by their unavailing efforts, they form the resolve to dismiss the painful subject until time, or a change in their circumstances, may remove their present embarrassments.

It might be supposed that salvation need only be provided and tendered, and men would at once accept the offer. Who can be unwilling to be saved? to have his sins pardoned? to be restored to the divine image and favor? and to become the heir of celestial bliss? Oh, how can men hesitate a moment to lay hold on eternal life, so dearly purchased, so kindly proffered, and so earnestly pressed on their acceptance? Yet they *do* hesitate. The feast of love is spread, and the invitation goes forth, "Come, for all things are now ready" but all with one consent make excuse. It is not that they do not need this provision; not that they do not desire to be saved, but because they have no relish for this spiritual food. They desire to be happy, but not to be holy; to be saved from hell, but not from sin; to share in the Christian's privileges, but not to submit to the Christian's sacrifices.

The young ruler went away from Christ sorrowful, because he valued the world more than he valued heaven. Felix stifled his convictions of duty, and dismissed the faithful preacher from his presence, because he was unwilling to renounce his sensual indulgences. Agrippa, though almost persuaded to be a Christian, refused to obey the dictates of his conscience, probably because he loved the praise of men more than the praise of God. Men are sometimes brought to a point where they manifest a willingness to give up everything that stands in the way of their salvation, but *one thing.* There is still some darling sin to which they cling, some self-denying duty which they will not perform; and that single obstacle shuts them out of the kingdom of heaven.

It is seldom that men are willing to avow the true reason for their postponement of attention to the claims of God. They will plead the want of time, the pressure of their worldly business, their inability to comply with the commands of God; their dependence on divine grace. But the true difficulty lies deeply imbedded within them—their inveterate opposition to God and holiness. But for this no sooner would the offer of salvation be made to them than it would be cordially embraced. We do not find them treating other matters, involving their interest, with such neglect. Offer to a sick man a remedy which he believes will cure his disease, will he neglect it? Hold out to a drowning man your hand to rescue him from his peril, will he refuse it? Spread your table before a man famishing with hunger, will he decline your invitation?

And why do not men as promptly avail themselves of the help proffered to them in the gospel? Why do they not at once accept the balm that can heal their spiritual malady? Why do they not lay hold of the arm stretched forth to rescue them from perdition? Why not crowd to the banquet of mercy, and partake of the bread of life that they may not die? Simply because their hearts are averse to the way of salvation made known in the gospel. Oh, what a state is this! No heart to love the infinitely blessed God! No heart that can be moved with gratitude towards a bleeding Saviour! No heart broken and contrite in view of crimes so numerous and aggravated! No heart to confide in one who is so entirely worthy of our confidence! How deeply fallen is man!—how unfit for all communion with God on earth, and for all blissful fellowship with him in heaven!

Yet such is the state of every unrenewed heart. Not only is there the absence of all true love to God, but there is positive *aversion.* It is only in view of this fact we can account for the reluctance which men everywhere manifest to fix their attention on divine things. "They did not like to retain God in their knowledge." "God is not in all their thoughts."

Reader! have you never discovered within yourself this aversion to sacred duties? Are you not conscious of a tendency to banish all thought of God and eternity? Why have you not to-day bowed your knee before the Most High in prayer? The throne of grace, sprinkled with atoning blood, is accessible, and you may approach it with the utmost freedom. God invites you near, and waits to answer your requests. Yet you keep at a distance. And why? Simply because you have no heart to pray—no relish for prayer—no desire for communion with God.

Will you be candid enough to admit this? The admission may be humiliating and painful, but we would hope that it may prove salutary. It may, at least, convince you of the deceitfulness of those excuses you are inclined to urge for your neglect of religion, and may disclose to you the real hinderance. It may also satisfy you that nothing is to be gained by delay; for if you cannot repent now, when can you repent? Time, so far from removing the difficulty, will only increase it. The infirmities of age may produce a change in your taste for sinful indulgences, but they will never eradicate from the heart its inveterate depravity.

CHAPTER III.

RELIGION A PRESENT OBLIGATION.

IF men are ever bound to become Christians, the obligation must be a *present* one. Thus runs the mandate of Heaven: "God *now* commandeth all men everywhere to repent." "Acquaint *now* thyself with him, and be at peace." "Choose ye *this day* whom ye will serve."

Whatever may be the nature of the duty enjoined, the obligation to immediate compliance is always either expressed or implied. Repentance, faith, submission, and prayer, are all present duties. Nor can a single passage be found in the Bible authorizing the delay of these duties *even for a moment.* Such license would be manifestly derogatory to the honor of God, and unsuited to the relations and circumstances of man. It would be a virtual abrogation of the divine law, and a connivance at sin utterly inconsistent with the divine character. If God has any claim on man, that claim must be supreme, and imperative. Not only does he require prompt obedience, but his demand is most urgent. He pays no regard whatever to the pleas you are in the habit of urging. In full view of all your supposed difficulties he calls upon you instantly to return to your allegiance, and embrace his offered grace. "How long halt ye between two opinions?" "Oh, that they were wise, that they understood this, that they would consider their latter end." "Turn ye, turn ye, why will ye die?"

Such is not only the call of his word, but also the call of his Spirit. "To-day, saith the Holy Ghost, if ye will hear his voice, harden not your heart."

And what is the voice of Providence? "Be

ye also ready, for in such an hour as ye think not, the Son of Man cometh."

"Time flies, death urges, knells call, Heaven invites, Hell threatens."—All cry in the ear of thoughtless, wayward man, "Whatsoever thy hand findeth to do, do it with thy might."

What possible plea, then, can the reader urge for procrastination? Will the requirements of God ever be more explicit? Will the tender of salvation ever be more urgent? Will the claims of your Maker ever be more reasonable? If it be your duty to love God at all, it must be your duty now; for never will he be more entitled to your love. If it be your duty to repent of sin at all, it must be your duty now; for the evil of sin is the same to-day that it will be hereafter. If it be your duty to confide in Christ at all, it must be your duty now; for he not only requires your present confidence, but he most richly merits it.

What can render it your duty to become a

Christian in advanced age, in sickness or in death, that does not render it your duty this instant? Is it that your danger may then be more imminent? But this is basing your obligation solely on a regard to your own safety. That obligation rests primarily on the authority of God, and the relation which you sustain to him as an accountable being. The present is emphatically *his* time. "Behold now is the accepted time; behold now is the day of salvation." He offers you salvation now, commands you to accept it now, and is just as willing you should accept it this moment as at any future time. You need not wait for God, for he has long been waiting for you—waiting to be gracious.

> "All the day long he meekly stands,
> The rebels to receive;
> And shows his wounds, and spreads his hands,
> And bids you turn and live."

My dear reader, there is infinite guilt as well as imminent danger connected with this delay. You may believe that you mean to repent at some time; but God is not thus to be put off. The whole life of the impenitent sinner is one of uninterrupted disobedience. Every day you are met by the call to repent, and every day that call is disregarded. It meets you on the sacred page, and in the sacred desk. It comes from the Spirit of all grace, and from the voice of your own conscience. It comes from the graves of the departed—from the ransomed in glory, and from the lost in despair. How loud, how solemn, how impressive that call; but, alas! how long, and how criminally neglected!

"Repent! the voice celestial cries;
No longer dare delay;
The soul that scorns the mandate dies,
And meets a fiery day.

"No more the sovereign eye of God
O'erlooks the crimes of men;
His heralds now are sent abroad,
To warn the world of sin.

O sinners! in his presence bow,
And all your guilt confess;
Accept the offered Saviour now,
Nor trifle with his grace."

"Give me an answer before you move."

Why Delay? p. 29.

When Popilius, by order of the Roman Senate, required Antiochus to withdraw his army from the king of Egypt, and he desired time for deliberation, the Roman ambassador drew a circle with his wand about him, and said, "*Give me an answer before you move.*" Such a circle I would draw around my hesitating reader, and in the name of Heaven's eternal Sovereign, I would say, "Give me an answer before you move." Now, while your eye is fixed on these pages—NOW, while the truth is pressed upon your conscience. It is not our message, we are delivering, but the message of God. We dare allow you no more time for deliberation than he allows. God is in haste, and man should be in haste too.

CHAPTER IV.

THE CHIEF END OF MAN.

It is a very common, but certainly a very erroneous impression, that religion is designed rather to fit men to die than to fit them to live. Under this delusion, multitudes defer the matter just as long as they think it can be done with safety or impunity. Time is spent in the service of sin; Eternity they hope to spend in the service of God. Though they live without prayer, by no means do they intend to die without prayer. They calculate that in their last moments they will themselves pray, and, perhaps, call in some Christian friend or minister to pray for them.

But without vital piety, a man is no more prepared to live than to die. He is no more qualified for earth than for heaven.

What is the chief end of man? For what purpose has he been created? Why has God endowed him with such noble faculties, and afforded him such ample opportunities, not only for receiving, but also for doing good? Infinite wisdom does nothing in vain. In all his works God must have some grand design: and what that design is we need not be at a loss to determine. All creation is intended as a monument to his praise, intended to manifest his glory. "The Lord hath made all things for himself." "The heavens declare the glory of God, and the firmament showeth his handy work." Animate and inanimate nature, rational and irrational beings, have all been called into existence to glorify the Great Creator. The very constitution of man indicates the design of his Creator. While he possesses certain properties, as to his physical organization, in common with other creatures, we find him endowed with faculties peculiar to himself, adapting him for purposes the most exalted. "There is a spirit in man, and the inspiration of the Almighty giveth him understanding." And why has God given him reason? Why has he given him conscience? Why has he made him susceptible of such noble affections? Can we suppose that all this is intended that he may act no higher part than the unintelligent creation, the beast that roams the forest, the bird that plumes its flight in the air, or the worm that burrows in the earth? Is it merely that he may gather his food, gratify his senses, and spend his life in unremitting toil to heap up treasure as transient as it is unsatisfying? Oh no; man was created for a higher and nobler purpose; and who can mistake that purpose? Man was made to serve and glorify God—glorify him not *passively* merely, as is the case with the inanimate and unintelligent creation, but *actively*, voluntarily, cordially. Why has God given us understanding, but that we may study the manifestation which he has made of himself in his works? Why has he given us the power of choice, but that we may prefer him above all things, and seek his glory as the highest good? Why has he given us affections, but that we may love him, and cleave to him, as our supreme portion and felicity? Why has he endowed us with conscience or a moral sense, but that we may distinguish between right and wrong, and follow our convictions of duty, as made known to us in his word? Why has he conferred on us the gift of speech, but that we may speak of his glorious perfections and works, and spread through the earth the honor of his name?

Such is the exalted end for which man has been made, and if he lives for any inferior object, he fails to answer the great design of his creation, and all his noble powers are perverted. He then becomes a mere blank, and better were it had he never been born.

How melancholy is it to see a creature capable of accomplishing such noble purposes, cleaving with his whole soul to the dust; seeking his highest happiness in the low gratifications of sense; wrapt up in his own selfishness, regardless both of the rights of God, and of the claims of humanity. Let us suppose that God had endowed the inanimate creation with the same power of volition with which he has endowed man. Suppose that in the exercise of that power, the sun refuses to shine, the showers refuse to descend, the fields refuse to bloom, and nature, instead of presenting a scene of loveliness, presents only a scene of desolation and barrenness. What heart would not be deeply affected in view of such defection? Who would not regret that the benevolent design of the Great Creator should thus be frustrated, and who would not expect that his works, refusing to answer the ends for which they were intended, would instantly be swept away, as unworthy of a place in the universe?

Or, take another case. What if the angels in heaven, whom God has formed for himself, and who are now employed in his praise and service, *should set themselves in hostility to*

God's government, and pervert those powers by which they now glorify Him, in dishonoring His name. Every heart now filled with celestial love, becomes inflamed with hatred; every harp is hushed in silence; the music of the skies ceases, and no sound is heard but that of discord and blasphemy. How shocking would appear to us such a change, and how ready would we be to conclude that beings, guilty of such a revolt, would be hurled, as were their former companions in bliss, down to the depths of wo and despair.

Now, men were as certainly formed to glorify God as were angels, and to refuse to do so, is just as criminal in the one case as in the other. You have no more right, dear reader, to withhold allegiance and homage to your Maker, than has Gabriel. The same obligations that bind him to the throne of heaven, bind you, and will bind you forever.

There can be no more serious charge brought against man than that which was once brought against a haughty monarch:

"The God in whose hands thy breath is, and whose are all thy ways, thou hast not glorified."

All creation is obedient to the voice of God, and subservient to his designs. The celestial orbs, in their unwearied revolutions, the valleys smiling with beauty, and the fields teeming with fruitfulness—the mountain, and the ocean, the feathered songsters that fill the air with their melodies, and the beasts that rove through the desolate waste—fire, hail, wind, clouds, and tempest, all speak for God, and answer, in their several ways, the end of their being. Man only refuses to glorify God—man, the lord of this lower creation—man, endowed with intellectual and moral powers that ally him to the very angels; man, in his pride and self-sufficiency, assumes the attitude of rebellion against his Maker's throne! All nature cries out against such a perversion of his powers. "The ox knoweth his owner, and the ass his master's crib; but Israel doth not know; my people doth not consider."

"The brutes obey their God,
And bow their necks to men;
But we, more base, more brutish things,
Reject His easy reign."

We are told of a distinguished lady in Scotland, devoted to the amusements and pleasures of the world, that, at a certain time, she was led to a serious examination of the first question and answer in the Shorter Catechism,

"What is the chief end of man?"

Answer.—"Man's chief end is to glorify God, and to enjoy Him forever."

The result was a deep conviction of her past guilt and folly, and the determination henceforth to consecrate her existence to the glory of her Maker.

Would that the reader could be persuaded to study that great question. Amid the hurry and bustle of the world, pause for one moment, and ask yourself: "Why has God brought me into existence? Why has he given me this body so fearfully and wonderfully made? Why has he bestowed on me these noble capacities of mind? What mission have I to perform on earth different from the animal that is left to the guidance of instinct? Surely I was not made merely to delve in the earth. My very nature aspires after something higher. God made me to glorify himself. Have I fullfilled the design of my being? Alas! God has scarcely been in my thoughts. My life has been wasted in sin and folly. My affections have been misplaced; my energies have been perverted, and I stand here only as a cumberer of the ground, inviting the speedy stroke of divine justice—fit only to be cut down, and consumed by the fires of divine vengeance."

And now, I ask, shall the future be spent as has been the past? Is it not time that you begin to live in reference to the great purpose for which life is given? Think, too, how much is to be done. Think of the millions who are perishing in sin, and who are calling for the word of life. This world, now in a state of revolt, is yet to be brought to a state of allegiance, and, in the accomplishment of this glorious enterprise, God permits each of us to take a part. It is your privilege not only to be saved yourself, but also to do something to save others. But whatever you do must be done quickly; the present generation will soon be gone, and you yourself will pass away with these millions to the judgment. Go, then, to-day and work in the vineyard. Why stand here all the day idle, when the labor is so great, and the season for activity will so soon close forever?

"Live, live for God,
And toil a world to save;
Live, live for God,
Nor heed the coming grave.
The time, the place, the way,
He knows them all;
Do well thy work to-day,
And wait his call."

"I have this day," said President Edwards, "been before God, and have given myself, all that I am and have, to God; so that I am in no respect my own. I can challenge no right in myself, in this understanding, this will, these affections. Neither have I a right to this body, or any of its members; no right to this tongue, these hands, these feet, these eyes, these ears; I have given myself clean away."

Such is the surrender which God demands of the reader. *Shall it now be made?*

CHAPTER V.

THE CLAIMS OF A REDEEMING SAVIOUR.

We now present to the reader a motive to immediate consecration to God the most tender and persuasive. It is derived not from the consideration of God as your creator, preserver, and governor, but as your merciful Redeemer. "Know ye not that ye are not your own? For ye are bought with a price; therefore glorify God in your body and in your spirit which are God's."

And what demand can be more reasonable? Here is an appeal both to your sense of justice and gratitude. If you belong to God by creation, how much more by redemption?

Dwell, for a moment, on the sacrifice which the Redeemer of our race has made for our salvation, and the immensity of that love which he has displayed in voluntarily offering himself up as our substitute, suffering the just for the unjust, that we might be brought to God.

Reflect on your sad and undone condition as a sinner—an outcast from God and heaven —exposed to the penalty of the violated law —your moral nature in ruins—plunged in a gulf of despair from which no human or angelic arm can rescue you. "But, when we were without strength, in due time Christ died for the ungodly."

When there was no eye to pity, his own eye beamed with commisseration; when there was no arm to save, his own arm brought salvation. And oh, how much did it cost to purchase our redemption! What a life of suffering—what a death of agony!

> "The ransom was paid down! the fund of Heaven,
> Amazing, and amazed, poured forth the price,
> All price beyond."

And all this, remember, was the fruit of

unmerited grace. God was under no obligation to make such a sacrifice for man. He might have left us to our helpless misery and ruin. Had the whole race been consigned to unending wo, his character would have remained unsullied, and his throne unimpeachable. All heaven would have approved of our doom, and our own consciences would have pronounced it just. It was love, pure, disinterested, boundless love that brought the Son of God from the skies, and led him to pour forth his blood for our redemption.

What pen is capable of describing the dimensions of that love? Who can measure its height, its depth, its length, its breadth? Who will attempt to describe what is so utterly indescribable? Who attempt to conceive what is so utterly inconceivable? Not until you can fully comprehend the dignity of the Saviour's person, the intensity of his sufferings, the depth of human apostacy, and "the glory which is to be revealed," can you comprehend the love of the divine Redeemer, who bought us with his blood. This is love that "passeth knowledge."

"God only knows the love of God."

And now, what does this Saviour ask in return for "love so amazing, so divine?" *He asks simply your heart;* he asks that you love him, confide in him, obey him. Is that too much? Could he require less? Would you give him less? Hear him as he urges his claim: "All this, O sinner, have I endured for thee; this shame for thee—this torture of body for thee—this anguish of spirit for thee—for thee a worthless worm of the dust—for thee who dost so richly merit only my eternal frown. And wilt thou refuse the acceptance of a salvation so dearly bought? Wilt thou withhold from me thy love, thy confidence, and thy service? Return unto me; for I have redeemed thee."

Oh, who can resist such an appeal?

"My Saviour! how shall I proclaim,
How pay the mighty debt I owe?

Let all I have, and all I am,
 Ceaseless to all thy glory flow;
Too much to thee I cannot give,
 Too much I cannot do for thee,
Let all thy love and all thy grief,
 Grav'n on my heart forever be."

It is related of a certain person, whom the efforts of Dr. Doddridge had released from the prison and the gallows, that on the day that had been appointed for his execution, he came to the door of his benefactor, where, falling on his knees, and the tears streaming from his eyes, he exclaimed: "Dear sir, I am come, before I die, to thank you—yes, every drop of blood in my veins thanks you; for you have had compassion on every drop. As long as I live I will serve you, and I will come every year from one end of the kingdom to the other to thank you."

Did that criminal express such gratitude towards a human benefactor, who had saved him from death temporal, what then should be our feelings towards that divine Saviour, who gave himself up as our ransom to save us from death eternal! Ten thousand hearts glowing with the warmest affection; ten thousand lives spent in the most self-denying service, would be but a poor return for love so rich, so costly, so unparalleled.

And can the reader be so ungrateful as to put off to the future the claims of such a friend? Does he not merit your best affections, your best energies, your best days? Will you give him only the dregs of your existence—a constitution worn out in sin—a mind enfeebled by age and disease? Will you take that heart which by right belongs to him, and devote it to the world? Will you employ that time which should be employed for him in the service of the adversary? You have no right to live a single moment unless you live for him—no right to speak, to act, to think but in reference to his will and glory. Oh, let me begin the eternal song of praise to my Saviour now. Let redeeming love be my theme living and dying; and when "this poor lisping, stammering tongue lies silent in the grave," let me then join the innumerable hosts in their rapturous hosannas to him that sitteth upon the throne, and to the Lamb forever.

Oh, there is something base beyond description in slighting this Saviour a single moment. This is the very climax of human guilt. In all the universe there is nothing to equal it. The reader may congratulate himself that his life has never been stained with any of those gross vices of which others may be guilty. But what sin can be marked with higher aggravations than that of treating with neglect the kindest and best friend of man?

During the late revival in Ireland, a lad who had found peace in believing, was asked what were the greatest sins that pressed so heavily on his heart, when under conviction. His reply was: "*I just did not believe in Christ.*" And could he have named any sin of greater magnitude? You might be guilty of any other, and of all other sins, but if you were free from this, you would be comparatively innocent. It is this sin, especially, of which the Holy Spirit convinces men, when they are brought to repentance. "Of sin, because they believe not on me." Should the reader, through the mercy of God, ever be brought to see himself in the light of divine truth, there is no sin that will bear with more weight on his conscience than that of having slighted the offer of a Redeemer's grace—refused to acknowledge a Redeemer's claims—"I would," says Dr. Payson, "as soon possess the heart of a murderer, of a traitor, nay, of a fiend, as a heart which turns cold and insensible from a crucified Redeemer—from bleeding, dying love—from the perfection of moral beauty and loveliness."

CHAPTER VI.

THE INTEREST AT STAKE.

IF religion were a matter of indifference or of secondary importance, delay in attention to its calls might admit of some justification; but if religion be anything, it must be everything; if it be needful, it must be the one thing needful; if it demands our attention at all, it demands our immediate attention. "It is no vain thing; it is your life"—*the life of your soul.* THE SOUL!—who can estimate its worth! Who can fully appreciate the importance of its salvation, or the fearfulness of its loss? All on earth is shadow. Decay is written on every object upon which we fix the eye. "All flesh is as grass, and all the glory of man as the flower of grass. The grass withereth, and the flower thereof falleth away." Kingdoms and nations that once acted a conspicuous part in the world's history, have long since passed away. One generation has quickly succeeded another, and the present will soon vanish with the past. These bodies, so fearfully and wonderfully made, have in them the seed of dissolution, and after a few more rising and setting suns, will mingle with their original dust. The places that now know us will then know us no more, and we shall no longer have any part in the transactions of this busy earth. "The heavens themselves shall pass away with a great noise, and the elements melt with fervent heat; the earth also, and the works that are therein shall be burnt up." But the soul of man holds on in its interminable existence, "amid the wreck of matter, and the crush of worlds." Creatures of yesterday, as we are, we have entered upon a career that will know no end. Millions of ages hence we shall be the same conscious beings that we are now; and in some portion of Jehovah's dominions, shall exist in a state of consummate bliss or wo.

Tremendous thought!

> "To think when heaven and earth are fled,
>   And times and seasons o'er,
> When all that *can* die shall be dead,
>   That I must die no more!
> Oh! where will then my portion be?
> Where shall I spend eternity?"

What question can be invested with greater importance to man than that which relates to his eternal destiny? I am to think forever, feel forever, act forever. But what will be the nature of my thoughts, my feelings, and my actions? Am I to be holy or sinful, happy or miserable? Am I to dwell in the life-giving presence of God, or wither under his eternal frown? Am I to be the companion of angels or of devils? Am I to swell the undying note of redemption to the Lamb, or take up the sad lamentation, "the harvest is past, the summer is ended, and I am not saved?"

Why should all our thoughts and anxieties be limited to this fleeting, transient life? Why should not man, as an immortal being, extend his views to the future, and determine, if possible, what is to be his allotment beyond the tomb? Is it not the dictate of wisdom to attend to those things first which are of the highest importance? Shall we care for straws, for bubbles, while we neglect interests of eternal moment? What are all the objects, the pursuits, the interests of time, compared with those of eternity? "What shall it profit a man if he gain the whole world, and lose his own soul?"

> "Oh! were the world one chrysolite,
> The earth a golden ball,
> And diamonds all the stars of night,
> One soul outweighs them all."

If, dear reader, your existence were limited to the present life, you would have nothing either to hope or to fear in reference to the future; or, were you an innocent creature, that future might present nothing appalling.

Death to you then would be but the passport to a higher and better state of existence—"the gate to endless joy."

But whose conscience does not accuse him of guilt? Who can confront his eternal Judge, and plead that he has never sinned? Who, if dealt with according to his deserts, must not meet with the sentence of condemnation? Your nature, exalted as it is, is a nature in ruins. Your soul, valuable as it is, is liable to be lost. The *soul lost!*—not annihilated; but doomed to an existence of eternal sinning and suffering—lost to God, lost to holiness, lost to happiness, lost to hope, lost irrecoverably and forever! What calamity can bear any comparison with this? Well might the universe be clothed in sackcloth, and utter one wail of anguish over such a disaster. The fearfulness of such a loss no pencil can describe, no heart can conceive. Heaven grant that neither the writer nor the reader may ever learn its import by experience.

Now, it was to save men from this ruin, that the Son of God poured forth his blood. He would not have shed it to save a thousand worlds, but he shed it for the soul of man. Here, then, we have his own estimate of the importance of man's salvation. Oh, how much is comprised in that one word—SALVATION!—Salvation from sin and from hell, "salvation with eternal glory"—not only deliverance from the greatest of all evils, but the possession of the greatest good—crowns of glory, palms of victory, songs of triumph, eternal progress in knowledge, holiness and bliss.

All this, and infinitely more than the writer can express, is now freely offered to you in the gospel; and shall interests so vast, so precious be neglected or be put off to a more convenient season? Shall all your efforts to secure these interests be crowded into the uncertain future? Better neglect everything else—better beg, starve, die, than neglect the great salvation.

What object can be of more immediate importance to a criminal under sentence of death than pardon? What more important to a drowning man than deliverance? "What must I do to be saved?" is emphatically *the great question;* and it should be to every man the first and all-absorbing question.

Men trifle with no other interests as they do with those of eternity. Everything else demands despatch, but "the vast concerns of an eternal state" are often left to the mercy of a single moment. A man is engaged in writing a letter. Suddenly he is startled by the cry of fire. Does he sit still, determined to fill up his sheet, regardless of the flames which are already encircling him, and the terrible ruin which impends over him? Important as he may deem the subject of his correspondence, it bears no comparison with the preservation of his life. In these circumstances self-preservation takes the precedence of every other consideration. And what object can be of greater moment to a poor condemned sinner than deliverance from the second death—escape from that unquenchable fire, which awaits all the finally impenitent and unbelieving?

We read that when Syracuse was taken by Marcellus, Archimedes, shut up in his closet, was so absorbed in solving a mathematical problem, that he was wholly unconscious of what was transpiring without. While thus absorbed in his private study, a soldier rushed in upon him, and bade him follow him speedily to Marcellus. "Stop," said Archimedes, "until I solve this problem." The soldier, enraged at his delay to obey the summons, drew his sword and struck him dead. You pity the folly of the philosopher, so absorbed in his studies at such a crisis, as to overlook the prior claim of self-preservation; and yet what an illustration have we here of the infatuation of thousands, who, in the eager pursuit of this world, neglect the interests of the future, and sacrifice, at last, their eternal all.

CHAPTER VII.

THE PRESENT ADVANTAGES OF PIETY.

AMONG other reasons that induce men to delay attention to the subject of religion, we may mention the prevalent delusion that it will interfere with *their present happiness.* They admit that it will make them happy in heaven, but they are not sure that it will render them happy on earth. It may be important to attend to it when they come to die, but they can see no special advantage to be derived from it while they live. Regarding it rather as a necessity than as a privilege, the matter is deferred until in their view, that necessity becomes extreme, and any further delay might prove hazardous.

What an evidence have we here of the blinding nature of sin! How truly is it recorded of men in their alienation from God, "the way of peace have they not known."

God made man for happiness, and has furnished him with ample means to obtain it; but it is our misery, no less than our sin, that we have forsaken the fountain of living waters, and have hewn out for ourselves broken cisterns that can hold no water. It is the universal inquiry of men, "Who will show us any good?" but "none saith, Where is God my maker, who giveth songs in the night?"

The world cannot satisfy the soul of man. It may minister to the wants of his animal nature, but his spiritual nature pants for some higher and more substantial good. Formed originally for communion with the Father of spirits, its lofty aspirations can be satisfied with no inferior enjoyment. It is only when it returns to God that it returns to its proper rest.

> "Give what thou wilt, without thee we are poor;
> And with thee rich, take what thou wilt away."

Man is a rational being, but how can reason be content to be chained down to sense? Man is an immortal being, how then can he feel at home in a world where all is shadow? The desires of man are boundless, how then can he be satisfied with the objects of earth and time? The soul of man was made not to feed on the husks of this world, but on angels' food.

Ever since the apostacy of our race, men have been seeking to be happy without God. The experiment has been made under the most favorable circumstances, but it has proved an utter failure. Solomon, the most distinguished monarch of his age, made it, and after availing himself of every earthly enjoyment, the melancholy conclusion to which he came was—"All is vanity and vexation of spirit."

Gœthe, the celebrated German poet, after gaining all the laurels the world had to give, wrote thus in his old age:—"They have called me a child of fortune, nor have I any wish to complain of the course of my life. Yet it has been notwithstanding but labor and sorrow; and I may truly say, that in seventy-five years I have not had four weeks of true comfort. It was the constant rolling of a stone that was always to be lifted anew."

Col. Gardiner, in the midst of a most successful career of sinful indulgences, was called "the happy rake;" but subsequently confessed, that, at that very time, he envied the happiness of a dog.

Byron could make out only eleven days of his life in which he had anything like enjoyment. "I am tired," he said, "and sick of every thing in life; there is no joy to be found on earth. I have often wished for insanity, anything to quell memory, the never-dying worm that feeds on the heart."

Sickened with the pleasures of earth, as he drew near the close of life, he wrote in melancholy strains:

"My days are in the yellow leaf,
The flowers and fruits of love are gone,
The worm, the canker, and the grief,
Are mine alone."

Shuter, the celebrated comedian, was at one time so affected by Whitefield's preaching, that hopes were entertained of his conversion. But the temptations to which his profession exposed him, soon swept away all his impressions, and disappointed the expectations of the pious. Speaking to the minister of Christ, he remarked: "The caresses of the great are exceedingly ensnaring. Lord E—— sent for me to-day, and I was glad I could not go. Poor things! they are unhappy, and they want Shuter to make them laugh."

Lord Chesterfield has borne one of the most emphatic testimonies on record, to the vanity of the world. "I have run," says he, "the silly round of business and pleasure, and I have done with them all. I have enjoyed all the pleasures of the world, and consequently know their futility, and do not regret their loss. I appraise them at their real value, which is, in truth, very low; whereas those who have not experienced them, always overrate them. They only see their gay outside, and are dazzled with their glare. But I have been behind the scenes.—When I reflect upon what I have seen, and what I have heard and done, I can hardly persuade myself that all that frivolous hurry, and bustle, and pleasure of the world, had any reality; but I look upon all that has passed, as one of those romantic dreams which opium commonly occasions; and I do by no means wish to repeat the nauseous dose for the sake of the fugitive dream."

I need not multiply such testimony. Thousands, surrounded with all the wealth and glitter of earth, are pining in anguish for some unknown good. "Even in laughter the heart is sorrowful, and the end of mirth is heaviness."

Hear now the language of a devout lady

who had made God her portion: "Where can I hope to meet with such joys as thy smiles have given me? Where can I find pleasure so sincere and unalloyed? When I have enjoyed the light of thy countenance, and the sense of thy love, has not all my soul been filled? Have I found any want or emptiness? Has there been any room left for desire, or any prospect beyond, besides the more perfect enjoyment of my God? Have not all the glories of the world been darkened, and turned into blackness and deformity? How poor, how contemptible have they appeared! or rather, have they not all disappeared and vanished as dreams and shadows in the noon of day, and under the blaze of the sunbeams? I have never found satisfaction in any thing but in God. I want nothing when I am possessed of thee; without thee I want all things. I have no joy but what flows from thee.—Secure of thee, nothing can terrify my soul; all is peaceful and serene within; eternal love, and immortal pleasure. I desire no more; imagination stops here, and all my wishes are lost in eternal plenty. My God! more cannot be asked, and with less I should be infinitely miserable."

Such has been the invariable testimony of all God's faithful servants as to the blessedness of true religion. Listen to their language as recorded by the pen of inspiration: "Whom have I in heaven but thee? and there is none upon earth that I desire besides thee." "Thy loving-kindness is better than life." "A day in thy courts is better than a thousand. I had rather be a door-keeper in the house of my God than to dwell in the tents of wickedness." "I will greatly rejoice in the Lord, my soul shall be joyful in my God." "I count all things but loss for the excellency of the knowledge of Christ Jesus, my Lord, for whom I have suffered the loss of all things."

Among the thousands who have devoted themselves to God, not one has been disappointed. In keeping his commandments they have met with great reward. The time was when, like those who are still strangers to grace, they sought their supreme happiness in the world; but never did it yield them what it promised. It allured only to deceive and to destroy.

"In search of enjoyment they wandered in vain,
With a void in their bosoms which nothing could fill;
For earth's gayest smile was succeeded by pain,
And the sweet cup of pleasure was bitterness still."

Would they exchange their present for their former state? Would they repeat the painful experiment which they once made, and give up the immortal hopes which they now indulge?

The religion of the gospel is a source of happiness at all times, but especially in the day of adversity and sorrow. "Man is born unto trouble as the sparks fly upward." Your mountain, my dear reader, may now appear to stand strong, and you may hope it can never be moved; but how soon may a sad reverse take place in your circumstances. Riches may make to themselves wings and fly away; friends may die; disease may invade your frame; and your prospects in life, now bright and joyous, may be darkened by impenetrable clouds. Where will you now look for support and consolation? The world, the fountain of your joys, is dried up; human sympathy, however grateful, fails to reach the deeply seated grief of your spirit; and if you have not made God your refuge, sad indeed must be your lot. Voltaire, notwithstanding the worldly honors with which he was loaded, remarked:—"Life is thickly sown with thorns, and I know of no other remedy than to pass quickly through them. The longer we dwell on our misfortunes, the greater is their power to harm us."

Such is the comfort afforded by infidelity. How different the feelings of the true believer. The eternal God is his refuge. His is a peace which the world can neither give nor take away. Whatever may be his afflictions, he receives them all as ordered by infinite wisdom and benevolence, and as a necessary part of that discipline by which he is fitted to enter upon eternal blessedness. "I know, O Lord, that thy judgments are right, and that thou in faithfulness hast afflicted me."

And now, dear reader, can you embrace this religion too soon? Can you be happy too soon?—make God your friend and portion too soon?—know the blessedness of pardoned sin too soon?—rejoice in the hope of immortal glory too soon?—To delay your duty, what is it but to delay your happiness? In devoting yourself to God you not only have nothing to lose, but everything to gain. Godliness has the promise of this life as well as of the life to come. It has been well said: "All the proper business of life would be better conducted—all the real enjoyments of life more relished—all the noble pursuits of life more successful, and all the poetry of life more lovely, were they combined with the vital godliness of a regenerated heart. Cowper did not cease to be a poet when he became altogether a Christian. The harp of Montgomery rose in sublimity as his heart ascended by the cross to the throne."

"Oh, taste, and see that God is good." You have tasted the bitterness of sin; come now and taste the sweetness of redeeming mercy. Come to the overflowing fountain of life and bliss. Feed no longer on husks, when there is bread enough in our Father's house, and to spare. "Wherefore do ye spend money for that which is not bread, and your labor for that which satisfieth not? Hearken diligently unto me, and eat ye that which is good, and let your soul delight itself in fatness."

CHAPTER VIII.

ALL THINGS ARE READY.

MORE than eighteen hundred years ago, when the Son of God expired on the cross, he cried, "IT IS FINISHED." The types and shadows of the former dispensation were now accomplished, the evil of sin was clearly exhibited, the violated law fully honored, and every obstruction to the free exercise of Divine mercy removed. God can now be just, and yet justify him that believeth. The fearful penalty of transgression may be remitted, and yet the throne of Heaven remain untarnished. Man's salvation is thus rendered *possible.* What we could not do ourselves, Christ, as our substitute, has done for us. By his one meritorious offering, he has made an ample atonement for the sins of the world, and brought in an everlasting righteousness for the free justification of all who trust in him. No man, therefore, need remain unsaved a single moment because salvation is not attainable. "All things are ready; come unto the marriage."

This salvation, purchased at the price of a Saviour's blood, is now most graciously *tendered.* Thus runs our high commission as the heralds of the cross: "Go ye into all the world, and preach the gospel to every creature."

Preach *what?* "THE GOSPEL"—the glad tidings of redemption through Christ.

Preach *where?* In "all the world," wherever man can be found, leaving no part of this habitable globe unvisited with the message of mercy.

Preach *to whom?* "To every creature," without a solitary exception, to individuals as well as to communities—all alike being involved in sin and ruin, and all alike needing the provisions of Divine grace.

To you, dear reader, has the word of this salvation been sent. You live not in a land of pagan darkness, but of evangelical light; a land of Bibles, of Sabbaths, and of sanctuaries. The sound of the gospel was almost the first sound that saluted your ears, the name of Jesus the first name with which you became familiar. Before your eyes Christ has evidently been set forth crucified; and in tones sweet and tender have you been invited to look to him and live. Pardon, purity, peace, salvation with eternal glory, have been tendered to you on the most reasonable terms—terms not only honorable to God, but precisely adapted to your own wants and circumstances. You are required not to work out a righteousness of your own, not to make an atonement by any sufferings of your own, but simply to believe and be saved. You have only to accept salvation with a penitent and trustful heart, and it is yours—yours the very instant you accept it.

And this tender of salvation is made to

you not once or twice, but *is renewed every day of your life.* The refusal of a single offer is a sin of such aggravation that we might suppose it would seal the doom of man forever; but so unwilling is God that you should perish, that he waits upon you with much long-suffering—waits to be gracious. Not a Sabbath returns, but you may hear the call of love; not a day elapses, but that call is repeated. Go back to childhood, and you were met with the free offer of salvation then. In youth, in manhood, down, perhaps, to old age, have you been followed by the invitations of Divine mercy.

But this is not all. It is an act of infinite grace for God to tender to you salvation; but he goes still farther—*he presses it upon your acceptance;* he stands pleading with you to accept it; he entreats, he implores you to accept it. Listen to his own emphatic words: "Turn ye; turn ye from your evil ways; for why will ye die?" "Oh, that they were wise; that they understood this; that they would consider their latter end!"

And what are the instructions he has given to his servants? "Go out, and compel them to come in." As though he had said: "Do not merely invite them, but urge them; ply them with every argument and motive. Hold on in your entreaties; take no denial." As ambassadors of Christ, we are sent to pray, *to beseech* men to become reconciled to God.

How deep is the solicitude which God thus manifests for your salvation! He is not simply willing that you should be saved, but his heart yearns for your salvation. Not a single means which he can consistently employ does he leave unemployed to prevail on you to accept his proffered redemption. He speaks to you by his word; he speaks to you by his ministers; he speaks to you by his church; he speaks to you by his providence; he speaks to you by his Spirit;—all with one voice crying in your ear, "Come to Jesus—come to heaven!"

And now, dear reader, if God has made such abundant provision for your salvation, and is so sincerely and earnestly desirous that you should accept it, I appeal to you, is it right, is it reasonable, that you should decline the offer? Must he still be put off with frivolous pleas and excuses? Is this the return you render to him for his kindness? Has redemption been purchased, and shall it still be refused? Is pardon tendered, and will you still remain under condemnation? Is there a fountain opened for sin and uncleanness, and will you still continue in all your defilement? Is the water of life flowing within your reach, and will you still refuse to partake of it? Is heaven opened, and will you still refuse to enter it?

What strange infatuation is this!

All things on the part of God ready, but man is not ready! The eternal Father ready, with open arms, waiting to welcome the prodigal home; Jesus the friend of sinners ready, standing at the very door of your heart with all the blessings of the blood-bought redemption; the Holy Spirit ready to seal you as the heir of salvation; the angels in heaven ready to hail with joy the first indications of sincere contrition; the glorified throng ready to tune their harps in praise over a new accession to the kingdom of God; the church of Christ ready to extend to you the hand of congratulation and fellowship;—and yet you still undecided!

What more reasonable than to suppose that salvation need only be offered, to be accepted. The great question, it would seem, must be—*Can* man be saved? But that is not the question now. *Will* he be saved? There is no obstacle in the way of his immediate salvation but what exists in himself. Upon whom then will rest the blame of his perdition? Oh, how awful to be brought so near the cross, so near the mercy-seat, so near heaven, and yet perish by DELAY!

CHAPTER IX.

NOTHING GAINED BY DELAY.

THERE are cases in which delay may be highly expedient and necessary. Time may thus be gained for deliberation, for the removal of difficulties, and eventually for more decided and efficient action. The skillful general delays, to avail himself of the most favorable crisis for a successful onset upon the foe ; the mariner, for the most propitious gale to waft him to his desired port ; the merchant, for the most auspicious season to purchase and to dispose of his goods. But in reference to the subject of religion, what possible advantage can be gained by delay ?

The reader may now feel that there are serious difficulties in his way, and may entertain the hope that they will hereafter be removed; but let him be assured that these difficulties, whatever they may be, so far from being removed or diminished by delay, will be greatly increased.

It is admitted that there will always be obstacles preventing the sinner's return to God, obstacles which Divine grace alone will ever enable him to surmount; but never will those obstacles be fewer than they are now. Every moment's delay only erects new and more formidable barriers, and renders your conversion less probable.

What do you hope to gain by delay? *Additional light?* Is not the path of duty already distinctly marked out? Have you not in your hands a complete revelation of the Divine will? Hear you not continually a voice from heaven, saying, "This is the way; walk ye in it?"

Do you *entertain doubts as to the truth and importance of Christianity?* Then, in the spirit of candor, carefully examine the claims which the gospel has on your confidence.

Take up your neglected Bible at once, and read it with the serious determination to arrive at the truth. Carry your perplexities to God in prayer, and implore him, as "the Father of lights," to remove them, and lead you in the way of salvation. "The meek will he guide in judgment; the meek will he teach his way."

The late William Wirt, Attorney General of the United States, and a candidate for the Presidency, was, for many years, an infidel; but subsequently acknowledged that he was never satisfied with the principles of infidelity, and never felt that it was safe ground to rest upon. At length he was led to examine the claims of Christianity as he would a question of Law, and after giving it the most thorough investigation, he came to the conclusion that it was divinely authenticated.

This conviction eventually resulted in his heartily embracing the plan of salvation as revealed in the gospel, and making an open profession of the religion of Christ.

But there are *mysteries*, you say, in the Bible which you first wish unraveled before you become a Christian. Mysteries undoubtedly there are, which no finite mind may ever be able to fathom; for "who by searching can find out God? Who can find out the Almighty to perfection?" But however much some of the doctrines of Christianity may be *above* reason, not one of them has ever been shown to be *contrary* to reason. Besides, these doctrines are revealed not as matters to be fully comprehended, but as matters of faith, founded on Divine testimony.

It is not necessary, in order to experience the benefits of Christianity, that you should fully comprehend its facts and doctrines, any more than it is necessary that you should understand the process of digestion in order that you may be nourished by your food, or the operation of a medicine in order that it may restore you to health. You have only to embrace with a hearty faith the great truths of Divine revelation, and however far beyond your penetration those truths may be, they will be made to you "the power of God unto salvation."

But why should the reader perplex himself with things above his comprehension, when his immmediate concern is with the question what as a sinner he must do to be saved. This is now your *great* concern, the concern which at present should absorb every other. What first of all you need to know is, how you may escape the penalty of sin, and be restored to the lost image and favor of God. On this point the Scriptures, surely, cannot be charged with obscurity. God has marked out the way of life so plainly that even a fool need not err. He has given you a book for the express purpose of solving the problem, how man can be justified before God; and no one who studies that book with prayer for Divine illumination, can fail to ascertain its meaning, and to be led into the knowledge of all essential truth.

Perhaps, however, the reader's plea is, not

the want of knowledge but of *conviction.* "My understanding," you say, "is enlightened. I know my duty. I am fully satisfied as to the truth of the evangelical system, and that there is salvation alone in Christ; but then, I have no deep sense of my fallen condition; I do not *feel* that I am a sinner; how then in my present state of mind can I embrace the offer of mercy?"

But will you urge that as an excuse which God regards as a crime? This very insensibility is a sin of peculiar enormity. It is not your misfortune, but the result of your own inconsideration and neglect. No man can seriously reflect on his condition as a sinner, his deep and ruinous depravity, and his constant exposure to death eternal, without the deepest solicitude. "My people do not consider." "No man repented him of his wickedness, saying, What have I done?"

No feeling! What a plea for a poor, guilty creature, lying under the curse of Heaven's violated law!

The reader may have more conviction than he is willing to admit—more than he is conscious of himself. Why these anxious thoughts about the future? Why this dread of a judgment to come? Why these inward upbraidings for neglected duty.

Conviction, indeed, is indispensable to conversion; but what degree of conviction it would be difficult to determine. There are some who, with comparatively little conviction, become Christians, while others whose sense of guilt and danger is overwhelming, still retain all their perverseness. It is not the depth of your conviction that will secure your salvation, but the actual surrender of your heart to the claims of the gospel. Yield to your present sense of obligation, and it will not be long before you will not only obtain fresh discoveries of the evil of sin, but also of the suitableness of Christ as a Saviour. You know that you are a sinner; why not then repent? You know that Jesus alone can save; why not in confidence commit your soul to him? You know that you are a needy, dependent creature; why not call on God for his aid?

What then do you hope to gain by delay? *Will the terms of salvation ever be changed?* Never. Why should they be changed? Are they not just such terms as are honorable to God and adapted to the condition of man—terms founded both on infinite wisdom and benevolence? God will save men in his own way, and in no other. The only alternative presented to sinners is, repentance or perdition, faith or damnation.

Will the *motives to piety ever be more forcible?* How can they be? What new truths shall be revealed? What more affecting appeals shall be made? Can you conceive of a heaven more glorious? of a hell more terrible? of love more tender? of obligation more sacred than you find presented in the gospel? You are pressed by motives drawn from time and eternity—motives that address themselves to your hopes and your fears, to your sense of justice and to your sense of gratitude, to your understanding, your conscience, and your feelings—motives which, were it not for the obstinate depravity of the human heart, would prove irresistible. Truths more solemn can never be presented to the mind of man; and if these truths fail to move him, his salvation is impossible. God will never reveal a law more holy, just, and benevolent; a Saviour more able and willing; a heaven of more surpassing grandeur and felicity; a hell of deeper gloom, and misery more terrible.

Will your heart hereafter become more *susceptible to the force of Divine truth?* You complain of the want of feeling; but is feeling to be produced by continued resistance? and resistance certainly there is, until the last moment of the sinner's rebellion and impenitence. By what process is it that some men have acquired such amazing moral insensibility? Blunted as may now be their feelings, they were not always so. The time was when a faithful sermon would send them from the sanctuary in tears; and when the sight of a corpse, or of the grave, would fill them with awe. Death, judgment, eternity, the love of Christ, and the wonders of redemption were themes that came home to their hearts with almost resistless power. But what a sad change is now visible. Their perceptions of Divine truth, once clear, have become darkened; their consciences, once awake, are lulled into a profound repose; and their hearts, once so readily moved, are past feeling. The cross is still exhibited; but they feel not its attractions. The love of a dying Saviour is still proclaimed; but their eyes remain unmoistened by a single tear. The law still utters its thunders; but they heed not its curses. The grave still speaks; but its summons awakens within them no alarm.

"Whence this change? Truth is not changed. The love of Christ is still the same. It is the same thing to die and to stand at the bar of God. No messenger has come from the invisible world to lower the terms of salvation. No one has come from heaven to tell them that its glories have passed away—that its crowns have faded, and its songs ceased. No one has come from hell to declare its fires quenched, and that its weeping and wailings are hushed forever. God sits on the same high and holy throne, supporting his government on the same eternal principles. All things in heaven and hell remain unchanged; the change is in themselves. They have resolved and re-resolved so often—they have wavered, and doubted, and hesitated so long, that they seem almost proof against any lasting impression."

I ask again—Will *your worldly circumstances* hereafter be any more favorable? I fear not. The convenient season of which you dream may never come. For such a season you have waited long, but waited in vain. It will always be inconvenient for a sinner to return to God. It is so even in childhood and youth, and much more in advanced life. No matter what may be your age or your circumstances, to break the cords that bind you to earth will require a decided and vigorous effort. "The kingdom of heaven suffereth violence, and the violent take it by force."

Will the influence of the Holy Spirit on your mind ever be more powerful? But what ground have you to entertain such a hope? For aught you know, that Spirit may already have gone as far as he can consistently, to subdue your perverseness; and, surely, if you resist the influence he is now exerting upon you, it does not become you to wait for any more powerful agency. The same depravity that leads you to oppose his present operations, might lead you to oppose his gracious designs were he to strive with you still more powerfully.

Will Christ ever be more willing to save you? You might as well question his ability as question his willingness. His heart yearns over you with the tenderest compassion, and his arms are wide open to embrace you the moment you fly to him for protection. What mean his invitations and promises? What mean his flowing tears and dying agonies? Why does he call after you with such melting importunity? Why stand pleading at the very door of your heart? Why has he spared you in the midst of merited wrath, and waited upon you with such amazing patience? What penitent has he ever spurned from his feet? What suppliant's cry has he ever shut out from his ear?

Reject the penitent! then would he falsify his own word, and oppose the grand design of his mission of love—then would angels suspend their songs, and hell shout in triumph. Trust in him, and you shall not be disappointed. Should you perish pleading with a truly penitent heart for mercy, you will be the first to perish thus.

Away with this spirit of unbelief! Take

him now at his word, and commit yourself into his hands.

> "Come, O my guilty brethren, come,
> Groaning beneath your load of sin;
> His bleeding heart will make you room,
> His wounded side will take you in;
> He calls you all, invites you home.
> Come, O my guilty brethren, come."

Would you render yourself *more fit* to come to Christ? What fitness does he require but simply that you feel your need of him, and then thankfully accept the salvation he so freely tenders. Attempt not first to save yourself, even in part, and then look to him to finish the work. "Ye are *complete* in him." He must be all or nothing. Come just as you are, "wretched, and miserable, and poor, and blind, and naked."

I have said that nothing will be gained by delay. I now add: much, *very much will be* LOST. You will lose all that time now wasted in sin, and all those opportunities for usefulness that are now afforded. You will lose that peace of conscience which results from a sense of pardoning mercy, and you will render your conversion daily less probable. Your sins, already numerous, are multiplying, demanding still deeper humiliation and penitence. "He who delays repentance a single day, has one day more to repent of and one day less to repent in." Delay, so far from diminishing the power of sin, only rivets the chains of the sinner more firmly.

It is an easy thing to crush an acorn, but let it grow to a tree, and no human arm may be able to uproot it. We all know the force of habit. It is a law of our nature that sinful habits grow with our growth, and strengthen with our strength. If you cannot break your grasp of the world now, when can you? If you cannot stem the influences that are bearing you on to perdition now, when can you? Every renewed act of transgression places you farther from God and heaven. Every moment that repentance is delayed, increases the reluctance to repent. "Can the Ethiopian change his skin, or the leopard his spots? Then may ye who are accustomed to do evil, learn to do well."

CHAPTER X.

THE DREADFUL RISK.

OBSERVATIONS on the shortness and uncertainty of life are so common, that it would seem needless to dwell on the subject. We are all ready enough to exclaim, "What shadows we are here. What shadows we pursue;" but how few realize the solemn truth; how few so number their days as to apply their hearts unto wisdom!

We need constantly to be reminded of our mortality, and with the Psalmist to pray, "Lord, make me to know mine end, and the measure of my days, what it is; that I may know how frail I am."

The delay of repentance is often founded on the presumption that death is yet at a distance. Strange is it to note how almost universal is this delusion. We see the sad ravages of the destroyer on every side. We live in a world of graves, and the mourners daily go about the streets, because man goeth to his long home. We witness the death of others, often their sudden death, and with saddened hearts bear their remains to the tomb; and yet "All men think men mortal but themselves; themselves they think immortal."

The hope of protracted life and of future repentance proves the ruin of untold numbers. Of all who, from a gospel land, have gone down to the world of despair, there were few who did not intend to repent. Death came to them too soon—came at an hour unlooked for—and, in a moment, their hopes and their souls perished together. Infidelity has destroyed its thousands, but *delay its millions.*

Did the reader believe that he was now spending his last day on earth, and that on its improvement was suspended his eternal well-being, with what eagerness would he seize upon the golden moments as they fly. No time must now be lost. What is done must be done quickly—done now or never. But to-morrow, you think, will be as to-day, and whatever else may demand despatch, the great interest, you presume, may be deferred to the future. Nothing can exceed the folly of this presumption. It is taking that for granted, which is of all things most uncertain.

> "In human hearts what bolder thought can rise,
> Than man's presumption on to-morrow's dawn?
> Where is to-morrow? In another world.
> For numbers this is certain; the reverse
> Is sure to none."——

Well has it been said that "by the circulation of the blood through the heart, in which motion is consumed and motion renewed every moment, the question is put about three thousand times every hour, and above a hundred thousand times every day and night of our lives, whether we shall stay in this world, or be in heaven or hell to eternity." Oh, what is life! "it is even a vapor that appeareth a little time, and then vanisheth away." "*A vapor;*" what more unsubstantial and fleeting, seen one moment, gone the next. Who will attempt to grasp it? Who can calculate on its continuance? Who build upon it his hopes? What is life? Life is "a tale that is told"—related, and then forgotten; a tale of joys and sorrows, of possessions and losses, of hopes and disappointments—a scene of continual fluctuation and change.—What is life? It is "as the *grass;* in the morning it flourisheth and groweth up; in the evening it is cut down and withereth." Life is what? A *dream*—how vain, how confused, how transient! Life is like a post, like the swift-sailing vessel, like the flight of an eagle through the air, a rapid stream; it is a hand-breadth, a span, a day, a watch in the night.

Such is the language by which the inspired writers represent the extreme brevity, the fleeting nature of human life. The longest life is but short. What are seventy or eighty years compared with eternity? And yet, ow small a portion of the human race are permitted to reach that period. How many are cut off in the midst of their days, and in the vigor of youth. How short the journey between the cradle and the grave.

What sad vacancies are made in the family and the social circle during a single year. It is computed that during that period more than thirty millions of our earth's inhabitants past away to the judgment. Death lurks continually in ambush. Go where you will, you have no security that his dart may not penetrate you the next moment. He is in your dwelling, in your shop, in your store, in your office; and to his summons there can be no resistance. He weighs no arguments, heeds no cries, admits of no parley, grants no reprieve. You may plead your youth; you may plead your pressing engagements; you may plead your worldly attachments;

you may plead your unfitness; but you plead in vain. Death may have singled you out as one of his earliest victims; ere you are conscious of his approach, his shaft may enter your bosom, and in an instant you may find yourself in the presence of your eternal Judge.

Listen to the voice of the departed—the voice of God's providence. A thousand graves utter the language of admonition and warning—a thousand graves call upon you in tones loud and impressive, to do what your hands find to do with your might.

Visit the depositories of the dead, and beneath how many sods repose the remains of those whose prospect of life was once as flattering as yours. Here lies one, who, though careful and troubled about many things, had sadly neglected the one thing needful. Often had she been admonished to choose that good part which would never be taken from her; but while she admitted the importance of the summons, the world still continued to engross her attention; she felt that she had no time or disposition to give to eternity any serious regard. She *meant* to repent; but with scarcely a moment's warning, her probation closed, and her spirit, unadorned with the robe of righteousness, entered upon its final destiny.

There lies the once enterprising merchant. Intent on his gains, all his plans were formed and prosecuted only in reference to the present. Suddenly he sickened and died. The world moved on as before, but no longer had he any part in the affairs of earth.

Beneath another hillock are interred the remains of a once industrious mechanic. His sole anxiety was to make provision for the support of himself and his family. As to the salvation of his soul; that, he seemed to think, was a matter of no immediate importance. The claims of the gospel had been repeatedly pressed upon him; but were continually evaded by the promise of a future recognition. But alas! he died as he lived, without God and without hope.

Here lies one who continued to add house to house, and field to field. His broad acres were so productive, that he knew not any longer where he might store his goods. The plan was formed to tear down his barns and build larger ones; and then to enjoy the fruits of his industry. But hark! what summons is that which comes from the throne of God? "Thou fool! this night thy soul shall be required of thee." His days are numbered, and he dies, having made provision for his body, but for his soul none.

Walk a few steps farther. Who lies there? There lies a youth who had enjoyed distinguished religious privileges; the child of Christian parents, and the subject of deep religious convictions. Many a time had he thought of yielding himself to God, but the season was always future. In the morning he left home in health; but he was carried back the same day a corpse; hurried by sudden death to the bar of God.

Oh, how little do we know what a day may

bring forth! To how many is the present day the last day, the present moment the last moment. While the reader is reflecting on death, thousands are experiencing it. Oh, write it upon your chambers, write it upon your possessions, write it upon the very tablet of your heart.—*Death is near, even at the door.* Patriarchs, prophets, Apostles, the word and the providence of God, cry aloud in the ear, "All flesh is as grass, and all the glory of man as the flower of grass."

And now I appeal to you, whether it is wise, whether it is safe to risk your eternal salvation upon the brittle thread of your present existence? Think of the great object for which life has been given, and for which it is prolonged; think of the results that are to follow man's probation—the mighty work which is here to be performed, and the momentous decisions that are here to be made; and who that has but one soul to save can venture the destiny of that soul upon the uncertainty of a future repentance?

A few years since a pastor made a pungent appeal to his hearers in reference to the danger of delay. "Will you," said he, "run the risk of losing your souls? Will you run the risk of losing heaven? Will you run the risk of perishing in your sins, and dying without hope?" At the close of the service, in passing down the aisle, a lady, deeply impressed with the appeal which had been made, said, in a low but earnest tone to a young lady of her acquaintance, "Can you resist such an appeal as you have just now heard? Will you venture to run the risk of losing your soul?" "Oh yes," she replied, in a thoughtless tone, "I will run the risk." In about a week after, the pastor was called to attend the funeral of a young person who had died suddenly. It proved to be the young lady who had ventured *to run the risk of losing her soul.*—Eternity will tell the rest.

A missionary in one of the Western States, once addressed a man of wealth on the importance of personal religion. The man assented to the truth; but evaded it, by the promise that he meant at some future and more convenient time to give the matter his serious attention. "Do you see," said he, "that spot of ground yonder? There I intend to build a house, and when that is finished, I shall turn my attention to religion." The missionary again visited the place; the house was not yet built, but the man was in his grave.

"*I have missed it at last.*" Such, said a gentleman at the Fulton street meeting in New York, were the words of a young man who had died the night before. They were addressed to his physician, who was sitting by his bedside, and who had just communicated to him the unexpected intelligence that he had but a short time to live. The young man looking up into the face of his physician with despair upon his countenance, exclaimed, "I have missed it—at last!"

"What have you missed?" "inquired the tender-hearted, sympathizing physician.

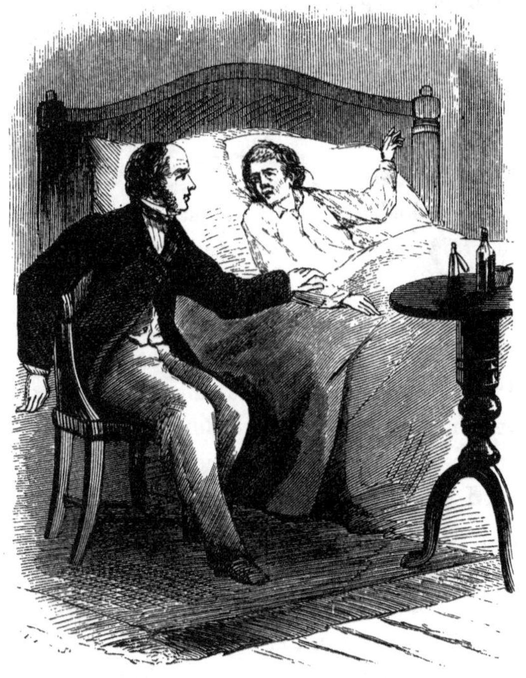

"I have missed it—at last."

Why Delay? p. 103.

"I have missed it—at last," again the young man repeated.

The doctor, not in the least comprehending what the poor young man meant, said, "My dear young man, will you be so good as to tell us what you ——?" The dying youth interrupted him, saying,

"Oh! doctor, it is a sad story—a sad—sad story, that I have to tell. But I have missed it!"

"Missed what?"

"Doctor, I have missed my salvation!"

"Oh! say not so. It is not so. Do you not remember the thief on the cross?"

"Yes, I remember the thief on the cross. And I remember that he never said to the Holy Spirit—"Go thy way. But I *did*. And now he is saying to me—'Go your way!'" He lay gasping a while; and looking up with a vacant, staring eye, said—"I was awakened, and was anxious about my soul a little time ago. But I did not want religion then. Something seemed to say to me,

Don't put it off—make sure of salvation. I said to myself, I will postpone it. I knew I ought not to do it. I knew that I was a great sinner, and needed a Saviour. I resolved, however, to dismiss the subject for the present. Yet I could not get my own consent to do it, until I had promised that I would take it up again, at a time not remote and more favorable. I bargained away, insulted, and grieved the Holy Spirit. I never thought of coming to this. I meant to have religion and make my salvation sure. And now 'I have missed it—at last!'"

"You remember," said the doctor, "that there were some who came at the eleventh hour?"

"My eleventh hour," he rejoined, "was when I had that call of the Spirit. I have had none since—shall not have. I am given over to be lost!"

"Not lost," said the doctor, "you may yet be saved."

"No—not saved—never. He tells me I

may go my way now. I know it—I feel it —I feel it here"—laying his hand upon his heart. Then he burst out in despairing agony, "Oh, I have missed it. I have sold my soul for a pin—a feather—a straw! Undone, forever!" This was uttered with such unutterable, indescribable despondency, that no words were said in reply. After lying a few moments, he raised his head, and looking all around the room for some desired object—turning his eyes in every direction—then burying his face in his pillow, he again exclaimed in agony and horror, "*Oh! I have missed it at last!*" and he died.

How awful to be thus ushered unprepared into the world of retribution; the last accents of mercy dying away upon the ear, and the spirit enshrouded in all the darkness of eternal gloom and despair!

Facts like the above might be multiplied. There is scarcely a pastor, who has been for any length of time in the ministry, who has not been called to witness similar scenes. I know there are thousands who die as they live. There are no bands in their death; but to what numbers is presented only a fearful looking for of judgment and of fiery indignation.

Oh, this procrastination! Well has it been denominated "the thief of time"—"the recruiting officer of hell."

> "It weaves the winding-sheet of souls,
> And lays them in the urn of everlasting death."

"*Too late! too late!*" is the piercing wail uttered by many a lost spirit—too late for repentance—too late for pardon—too late for salvation.

There are some men who are too late in almost every thing—too late for the cars—too late for the boat—too late at church—too late in meeting their engagements, and alas! too late in securing the eternal prize. There is such a thing as being one day, even one moment too late. On the morning of that day in which Cæsar was murdered in the

Senate house, he received a letter informing him of the design of his conspirators; but neglecting to read it, he lost his life.

It is said to have been a custom among the ancient Romans, when they attacked a city, to hoist a white flag at the gate. If the enemy surrendered, while the flag was there, their lives were spared; if not, a black flag was raised, and every one was slain. Dear reader, the white flag now floats before you. Surrender, and you are pardoned; refuse, and by to-morrow you may perish.

"To-day the Saviour calls!
Ye wanderers, come;
O ye benighted souls,
Why longer roam?

"To-day the Saviour calls!
For refuge fly;
The storm of vengeance falls,
Ruin is nigh.

"The Spirit calls to-day!
Yield to his power;
Oh! grieve him not away;
'Tis mercy's hour."

CHAPTER XI.

DIVINE ABANDONMENT.

"WO ALSO TO THEM WHEN I DEPART FROM THEM!" A more awful denunciation than this can hardly be found on the pages of the Bible. To be abandoned by Him whose favor is life, and whose frown is death, is the very consummation of human misery.

And when is this dreadful sentence executed upon the incorrigible? At death? Unquestionably it is. No acts of pardon are passed beyond the grave; no invitations of mercy are extended to those who have passed to the world of spirits unredeemed. Hence the general dread which is felt in prospect of immediate and sudden dissolution.

It is, however, a solemn fact that man's

day of grace may terminate long before the close of life. The limits of that day are fixed by infinite wisdom, and terminate whenever God in his sovereignty sees fit. The withdrawment of his gracious influence from the heart, as certainly decides the destiny of man, as his immediate citation to the judgment. Let those who are postponing the great interests of eternity to the future seriously ponder the truths contained in the pages of this chapter.

The salvation of man is wholly dependent upon the agency of the Holy Spirit. We can no more be saved without the influence of the Spirit than without the atonement of Christ. A Saviour may die, an ample atonement may be made, and a free salvation may be tendered; but not a soul will accept the offer of mercy unless made willing by the Spirit. It is the Spirit who convinces the world of sin, who takes away the heart of stone and gives a heart of flesh. It is the Spirit who guides the believer into all truth, comforts him in all his sorrows, and seals him unto the day of redemption. All holiness in fallen man is "the fruit of the Spirit." Not one gracious affection would he ever exercise, were it not wrought in him by the power of the Holy Ghost. The truth may be exhibited with ever so much clearness and fullness; but it is powerless either to convince or to convert, unless accompanied by a Divine influence.

The gracious influence of the Holy Spirit may, at any time, be withdrawn, and the sinner may be left to his own chosen course of sin and ruin. "My Spirit shall not always strive with man." Hence the solemn admonition, "Grieve not the Holy Spirit." "Quench not the Spirit." It is recorded of sinners of a former age, "they rebelled and vexed his Holy Spirit; therefore he was turned to be their enemy, and he fought against them." Isaiah lxiii. 10. There is such a thing as being given over to our own heart's lust—given over to a reprobate mind, given over to blindness of mind and hardness of heart.

Esau, we are told, for one morsel of meat sold his birth-right, and afterward when he would have inherited the blessing, he was rejected; for he found no place of repentance, though he sought it carefully with tears. Heb. xii. 16, 17. How bitter was the lamentation of Saul when God left him to himself: "I am sore distressed; for the Philistines make war against me, and God is departed from me." 1 Samuel xxviii. 15. And how affecting the exclamation of Jesus, as he behold the doomed city of Jerusalem, and wept over it: "If thou hadst known, even thou, at least in this thy day, the things which belong unto thy peace! but now they are hid from thine eyes." Luke xix. 42.

If men, in former days, were thus abandoned by God, then may they be abandoned by him now. In this age of evangelical light, and religious revivals, there is imminent danger of grieving away the Holy Spirit.

Just in proportion to the power with which he strives, is the guilt and hazard of resistance. There can be no doubt that multitudes, yet out of their coffins, have already decided their eternal doom. The Spirit who once strove with them strives with them no more; and however long their life on earth may be protracted, they live only to treasure up wrath against the day of wrath. No means employed to bring them to repentance, will ever produce the effect. Sermons are preached to them in vain; prayers are offered for them in vain; tears are shed over them in vain. The kingdom of God may be brought nigh unto them; the whole community around them may be aroused under the mighty movements of God's Spirit, and converts may be multiplied by hundreds and thousands; but they still continue to reject the counsel of mercy, and perish at last.

Who these unhappy beings are, it is not our prerogative to determine. We may give up no man while he is this side of the grave.

We may cherish the hope that even the most obdurate may yet be brought to repentance; but our hope may well be mingled with fear and trembling.

How long the Spirit will continue to strive with the perverse heart; at what moment he may suspend his gracious influence, is one of those secret things which belong to him. As his influence is wholly unmerited, he may prolong or he may terminate it, as in his infinite wisdom he may deem proper. He may pursue the sinner for years, or he may abandon him the next moment. With some he strives until the close of life; some he follows to advanced age; some to middle life; and, in numerous instances, we have reason to believe, he abandons the soul even in youth.

The late Rev. Herman Norton records the following affecting instance. Often have I listened to its recital from his own lips.

An aged procrastinator, taking the servant of God by the hand, said: "Sir, do you think there is any mercy in heaven for a man who has sinned more than eighty years?"

"There is mercy," I replied, "for those who repent of sin, and believe on the Lord Jesus Christ."

Still pressing my hand, while tears were flowing down his wrinkled cheeks, and his frame trembling, he more earnestly renewed his inquiry, "My dear sir, do you believe that God will forgive a man who has rebelled against him eighty-one years in this world?" Before a word was uttered in reply, he cried out in agony, "I know I shall not be forgiven! I shall die in my sins!"

"This caused me to ask how he knew or what induced him to believe that God would never have mercy on him."

He replied, "I will tell you, and disclose what I have never uttered to any human being. When I was twenty-one I was awakened to feel that I was a sinner. I was then intimate with a number of young men, and was ashamed to have them know that I was anxious for my soul. For five or six weeks I read my Bible, and prayed every day in secret. Then I said in my heart, one day, I will put this subject off until I am married and settled in life, and then I will attend to my soul's salvation. But I knew that I was doing wrong.

"After I was settled in the world, I thought of the resolution I had made, and of my solemn promise to God then to make my peace with him. But as I had no disposition to do so, I again said in my heart, I will put off this subject ten years, and then prepare to die.

"The time came, and I remembered my promise ; but I had no special anxiety about my salvation. Then did I again postpone and resolve that if God would spare me through another term of years, I would certainly attend to the concerns of my soul. God spared me, but I lived on in my sins ; and now I see my awful situation. I am lost.

"I believe that I sinned against the Holy

Ghost when I was twenty-one and that I have lived sixty years since my day of grace was past. I know that I shall not be forgiven."

"When asked if we should pray with him, he replied, 'Yes; but it will do no good.' So fearfully certain was he of destruction! He continued in this state for weeks and months. All attempts to urge him to accept of salvation were in vain; this blighting sentiment was ever first in his thoughts—'It will do no good.' His feelings were not contrition or repentance for sin, but the anticipation of wrath to come. And in this state he died."

This is only one of numerous instances that might be mentioned, illustrating the danger of delay, and of resisting the influence of the Holy Spirit.

"There is a time, we know not when—
A point, we know not where,
That marks the destiny of men
To glory or despair.

"There is a line by us unseen,
Which crosses every path—
The hidden boundary between
God's patience and his wrath.

"To pass that limit is to die—
To die as if by stealth;
It does not quench the beaming eye,
Or pale the glow of health.

"The conscience may be still at ease,
The spirits light and gay;
That which is pleasing still may please,
And care be thrust away.

"But on that forehead God has set
Indelibly, a mark,
Unseen by man; for man as yet
Is blind, and in the dark.

"And yet the doomed man's course below,
Like Eden, may have bloomed;
He did not, does not, will not know,
Or feel that he is doomed.

"He feels, he knows that all is well,
And every fear is calmed;
He lives, he dies, he wakes in hell,
Not only doomed, but damned."

No procrastinating sinner can tell how soon he may cross that mysterious line which bounds his probation. He may be within a single step of it. The very next act of transgression, or the rejection of the next offer of salvation, may place him beyond the reach of hope forever. Men go on in sin, presuming that they may obtain mercy when they please; but God is not thus mocked. When their time comes, God's time may have gone beyond recall.

And let it be observed, that to reach this awful crisis it is not necessary to be guilty of any open immorality, or to embrace any infidel sentiments. Only refuse to cherish the Spirit's influence, and to comply with his gracious call, and you may grieve him away, never more to return. His departure may be the result of a long and obstinate resistance of his strivings, or it may immediately follow one determined effort of the mind to get rid of conviction.

The sinner, awakened to a sense of his peril, begins to inquire what he must do to be saved. His duty is plainly set before him, and he is urged at once to perform it. There are times when he is almost persuaded to yield; but still he hesitates. There is still some favorite indulgence which he is unwilling to renounce, or some cross which he is unwilling to bear; at length, he forms the desperate resolve, to put off the matter to some indefinite or fixed period in the future, and to banish all his anxiety for the present. His mind is now relieved, and a calm follows which is the precursor of an eternal storm. God has departed from him, and with rapid strides he now wends his way to final ruin.

Oh, there is something awful beyond description in this departure of the Spirit. It closes the door of mercy against the sinner forever. Perhaps he is cut off suddenly, and hurried before the tribunal of God; or if spared for a time, he "resembles *the leafless girdled oak,* stretching its broad arms towards heaven only to invite God's lightning to rive it into a thousand atoms."

In the language of Dr. Doddridge we may

say to the procrastinating sinner: "If you delay any longer, the time will come when you will bitterly repent of this delay, and either lament it before God in the anguish of your heart here, or curse your own folly and madness in hell!—yea, when you will wish that, dreadful as hell is, you had rather fallen into it sooner than have lived in the midst of so many abused mercies, to render the degrees of your punishment more insupportable, and your sense of it more exquisitely tormenting."

The state of *the awakened, undecided* sinner is peculiarly critical. He may now be receiving his last call of grace; and his present state of mind must either issue in his salvation, or in more aggravated guilt and condemnation. A few hours may be followed by a most marked change in his feelings. Oh, trifle not with the tender wooings of Divine love. The blessed Spirit comes to your heart, not to torment you before the time, but to seal you unto the day of redemption. He wounds only to heal; he discloses to you your misery only that he may reveal to you an all-sufficient remedy. Grieve him not by your resistance or neglect. *Yield! this moment yield* to his benign influence; and he who has convinced you of sin will also prove to you a comforter and sanctifier.

"Delay not, delay not; the Spirit of grace,
 Long grieved and resisted, may take its sad flight;
And leave thee in darkness to finish thy race—
 To sink in the gloom of eternity's night."

CHAPTER XII.

THE GOLDEN SEASON.

> "There is a tide in the affairs of men,
> Which taken at the flood, leads on to *heaven*;
> Omitted, all the voyage of their life
> Is bound in shallows and in miseries."

WITH this accord the words of Solomon: "To everything there is a season, and a time to every purpose under the heaven;" and it is the dictate of wisdom to improve the most favorable periods to avert any impending evil, or to secure any desired good. In reference to man's salvation, YOUTH may emphatically be denominated *the Golden Season.*

It is the season which, of all others, is attended with *the fewest obstacles;* both as regards man's external circumstances, his natural constitution, and his moral condition.

Your mind, my young friend, is now unencumbered with those engagements and anxieties which commonly distract us in after life. The present may be a season of leisure, affording you the most convenient opportunity for reading and religious culture. Now, too, your constitution may be vigorous, your affections warm, your memory retentive, your conscience tender, and your heart far more impressible than at any future period. Now the Holy Spirit may be striving with peculiar power, and the means of grace may possess peculiar energy. Habits of sin may not yet be formed, and your heart may not yet have become callous to the appeals of Divine truth. Never, therefore, will there be a period when you will possess equal advantages to secure the Divine favor. "I love them that love me, and they that seek me early shall find me."

I know that the youthful heart, unchanged by Divine grace, is a sinful heart. I know, too, that nothing but that grace will ever effectually eradicate its deep corruption; yet it is entirely in accordance with the Scriptural doctrine of the Spirit's agency to say, that the conversion of some sinners is attended with greater difficulties than the conversion of others. That agency is adapted to man's nature and circumstances, and in proportion to the dominion which sin holds over the mind, is the display of the Spirit's power in renewing it, and the effort it may require to press into the kingdom of God.

A minister once made a most solemn appeal to the young. As he descended from the pulpit, at the close of the service, he was met by an aged man, who, extending his hand to him, said, with deep emotion, "I would give worlds if I could be placed where I was when I was twenty years old."

Early piety is *peculiarly acceptable and honorable to God.* In all ages of the world he has manifested a special regard for the young. A considerable portion of the Sacred writings is particularly designed for their instruction and improvement. He has required parents early to dedicate their children to his service, and to bring them up in his nurture and admonition. He has made it the duty of his ministers to feed the lambs; to exhort young men to be sober-minded, and he has ever been pleased to bestow upon youthful piety marks of special approbation and honor.

Joseph loved and honored the Lord at an early age, and from his history we find that the Divine favor attended him in all his subsequent life. Hated and sold by his brethren, the providence of God watched over his steps, raised him to a post of distinguished honor, endowed him with supernatural powers, and made him the happy instrument of preserving his father's family and a whole nation, during a long and distressing famine.

Samuel was early dedicated to God; and as he grew up, became not only eminent for his piety, but also for his endowments and usefulness.

The early piety of David also secured for him the special favor of Heaven. Though once a shepherd's boy, he afterwards became a king and a prophet, and the sweet Psalmist of Israel.

Josiah, it is supposed, became pious at the age of sixteen, and God honored him by making him the instrument of a glorious reformation, and also of averting the most terrible judgments.

John the Baptist appears to have been made a subject of sanctifying grace from his earliest childhood, and upon him was conferred the distinguished honor of heralding the appearance of the Messiah.

Timothy from a child knew the Holy Scriptures, and early walked in the steps of his pious ancestors; and both his piety and his usefulness are spoken of in terms of the highest commendation, "I have no man," says the Apostle, "like-minded, who will naturally care for your state."

And who are they that, in subsequent ages,

have commonly been most honored in advancing the kingdom of God? Have they not been those who have devoted to God their childhood, and their youth? Read the memoirs of Watts, of Doddridge, of Baxter, of Brainerd, of Martyn, of Edwards, and many distinguished females, Lady Jane Gray, the Countess of Huntingdon, or our own Harriet Newell,—all of whom were converted in early life. Look over the list of our modern ministers and missionaries, and it will be found that, with few exceptions, they consecrated to God the days of their youth. Of five hundred and seven individuals who, in 1834, were members of Theological Seminaries in the United States, about four-fifths were hopefully converted when under twenty-one years of age.

Under the former dispensation God required the first-born of man, the first-born of beasts, and the first-fruits of the earth for himself; and if you wish to offer to him an acceptable sacrifice, give to him the first of your days.

> "A flower when offered in the bud,
> Is no vain sacrifice."

If God merits any return from those upon whom he has lavished his favors, then must he merit your *best* return, your best faculties, your best affections, your best days—not the infirmities and decrepitude of age, but the buoyancy of youth, and the vigor of manhood. Waste not your energies in the service of sin, and then present the miserable dregs of enfeebled faculties, and of a broken-down constitution to the God of heaven. How much more generous and honorable to devote to him the gold than the dross, the harvest than the mere gleanings. Admitting that you should consecrate yourself to him in advanced life, what reason will you have to be ashamed of your offering, and what bitter regrets will you feel that you can offer to him no more suitable return. An old man of seventy-six once remarked: "I did not become interested in religion till I was forty-five, and I have often to tell God I have nothing to bring him but the dregs of old age."

Early piety, my young friend, will be attended with *peculiar advantages.* It will secure to you every needful *tenporal* blessing. The God who feeds the young ravens when they cry, and who clothes the fields with verdure and beauty, will surely not be unmindful of the wants of those who serve and confide in him. Having sought, *first,* the kingdom of God and his righteousness, you have the promise that all other things shall be *added* unto you.

True piety will *preserve you from the influence of temptation.*

Every period of life has its trials and dangers; but, perhaps, there is no period more perilous than that of youth. Now it is that the world presents itself in the most fascinating form. Now the natural ardor of your spirit may render you an easy prey to those scenes of gayety, pleasure, and dissipation which are everywhere spreading their concealed snares. You tread upon enchanted ground, and your very inexperience tends greatly to enhance your danger. You know, as yet, but little either of the world or your own heart. Your susceptibility of character, favorable as it may be to the influence of Divine truth, renders you proportionably liable to the influence of error.

Human life is a voyage, a voyage to eternity. The sea you have to navigate looks smooth and inviting; but it is filled with shoals, rocks, and quicksands. On that sea you have now embarked, perhaps without line, compass, or chart. Oh, how much do you need a pilot and protector. "Wilt thou not," says the Almighty, "from this time cry unto me, My Father, thou art the guide of my youth?" Look around and see the sad wrecks of ruined character, and blighted hopes that everywhere meet your eye. How many youth whose moral principle once appeared as firm as yours, have plunged themselves into irrecoverable ruin. Your security is in God alone. It is only when his arm holds you up that you are safe. Left to yourself the natural inclination of your heart would lead you to break away from all the early restraints that may have been thrown around you, and abandon yourself to every species of vice and folly.

The fact that religion will prove to you *a source of present happiness,* also commends it to your early choice.

I know that it is difficult to convince you of this truth. Serious piety may now be painted with gloom, while the way of transgression appears smooth and inviting. Be assured that this is all illusion. Never can you attain that happiness for which you were made, and for which you pant, but in the enjoyment of your forsaken God. Search creation through, and where can it be found but here? Wealth says, "it is not in me." Honor says, "it is not in me." Pleasure says, "it is not in me." Thy favor, O God, is life, and thy loving-kindness is better than life.

The unanimous testimony of all who have tried the service of God is that "wisdom's ways are ways of pleasantness, and all her paths are paths of peace."

"I have been," says a pious man, "in different courses, and have sought for happiness in different paths. I have sought it in mirth, in gayety and amusement. I have sought it in plans and purposes of ambition, and in the imagination of schemes of worldly aggrandizement and honor. I have sought it in the occupation of study, conversing on the page of history with generations that have gone, or mingling in the magic enchantments of poetry, or attempting the more laborious pursuits of intellectual inquiry; and I have sought it in the service of God. And *here* the craving appetite has found its food, and *here* the restless and anxious heart has found its peace and joy. Like the philosopher of old, but in an application far more exalted,

I can say, 'I have found it, I have found it!' In the service of God I am happy, and if I served him more, I should be happier still. To be as once I was, I would not for all the gold of every earthly mine, or all the gems of every ocean cave."

Oh that you would be persuaded to make the same trial. Religion will do for you all that it promises—do for you what nothing else can do. It will give you dominion over sin; it will calm the turbulence of passion; it will quiet the clamors of conscience; it will impart to you victory over death, and will open to your view the prospect of unfading glory. If happiness can be found anywhere, surely it must be found here.

You may now think that you can dispense with these enjoyments and consolations, but the time will come when you will feel that you need them.

While in the morning of life, everything wears the aspect of pleasure. You dream not of sorrow. Buoyant with hope, to-morrow you say, shall be as to-day, and much more abundant. But how quickly may all these enchanting prospects fade from your view. Health may now sparkle in your eye, and your spirits may be as gay as the morning; but that frame, now so vigorous, may soon be wasted by disease, and be turned to corruption. Those friends with whom you are now surrounded, and from whose society you derive no inconsiderable portion of your happiness, may be torn from your embrace, and buried out of your sight. And whither, in the hour of adversity, of bereavement, of sickness, and of death, will you flee for consolation, if you have not made God your refuge? Who but he can pour the healing balm into your bleeding bosom? Who but he can sustain you when all earthly dependences fail? Who but he can light up the valley of death, and enable you to descend in peace and triumph to the tomb? Possessed of him, you possess a treasure permanent and satisfying. He is "a friend that sticketh closer than a brother." The smile of his face can dissipate the thickest gloom, and impart to you a peace which the world can neither give nor take away.

Early piety will also be *favorable to high spiritual attainments.* Instantaneous as is the transition from a state of nature to a state of grace; the work of religion is not the work of a day. In regeneration it begins; in sanctification it is carried forward and perfected. "The path of the just is as the shining light, that shineth more and more unto the perfect day." Do you wish to become eminently pious, then you must become pious early. The sooner you enter upon the service of God, the more time and opportunity will you have for growth in knowledge and grace. "Those that are *planted* in the house of the Lord, shall *flourish* in the courts of our God; they shall still bring forth fruit in old age." Should the providence of God spare you to advanced life, what unspeakable gratification will it afford to review the way by which you have been led—to recount not only the trials through which you have passed, but also the supports you have received.

Dimness may now come over your vision, and the glory of earth may fade from your view; but by the eye of faith you look forward to "brighter scenes in heaven." Your ears may become deaf to the sweetest melodies of earth, but you continue to hear "the still small voice" of God saying, "Fear not, thou art mine; I have redeemed thee." The knowledge of the past may fade from your memory, but the law of God remains written on your heart, and whatever else you forget, never can you forget him who is all your salvation and desire. Your strength and your heart fail; but God is the strength of your heart, and your portion forever.

And then the earlier you enter upon the service of God the greater, in all probability, will be your happiness, not only in this world, but also *in the world to come.* All the redeemed will be perfectly happy; but all will not be equally so. As there are degrees of grace on earth, so will there be degrees of glory in heaven. God, we are assured, is not unfaithful to forget our work of faith, and our labor of love. "They that be wise shall shine as the firmament, and they that turn many to righteousness as the stars forever and ever." What a motive does this furnish to early piety. The sooner you enter into the vineyard of God, the more can you accomplish. Saved yourself, you may also become the honored instrument of saving others. Who does not aspire after the exalted privilege? Who can be content to go to heaven alone? Who, as he enters there, would not have some to greet him as his benefactor on earth, and rise up to call him blessed?

"If grief in heaven might find a place,
And shame the worshiper bow down,
Who meets the Saviour face to face,
'Twould be to wear a starless crown.

"To find, in all that countless host,
Who meet before the eternal throne,

Who once, like us, were sinners lost,
Not one to say, 'you led me home.'

"Oh, may it ne'er of me be said,
No soul that's saved by grace divine,
Has called for blessings on my head,
Or linked its destiny with mine."

But there is another aspect, my young friend, in which we must now present this matter.—*Should you neglect religion in youth, there is an awful probability that you will continue to neglect it until it be too late.*

The period of youth is a most critical period—the period that commonly moulds our destiny both for this life and the life to come. Conversions among the aged, and even the middle-aged, are comparatively rare. Here and there you may see a veteran in sin bowing in penitence at the foot of the cross; but the vast majority of the subjects of renewing grace are to be found among our children and youth. When God poured out his Spirit upon the Jews in the wilderness, it was not upon the aged but the young. While the fathers, who had been noted for their long abuse of the Divine goodness, were passed by, he visited their offspring, and from them raised up a seed for his service and glory. And thus it has been in all subsequent revivals.

The late Dr. Bedell, of Philadelphia, once said in a sermon to young men, "I have now been nearly twenty years in the ministry of the Gospel, and I here publicly state to you that I do not believe I could enumerate three persons over fifty years of age whom I have ever heard ask the solemn and eternally momentous question, 'What shall I do to be saved?'"

Of fifty-five who, on one occasion, made a public profession in the church of which the writer is pastor, not more than nine had passed the age of twenty, and not more than five the age of twenty-five.

Dr. Spencer makes the following observations:—"I once made an examination in respect to two hundred and fifty-three hopeful converts to Christ, who came under my own observation, at a particular period. Of these two hundred and fifty-three, there were converted,

"Under 20 years of age, - -	138
"Between 20 and 30 years of age,	85
"Between 30 and 40 years of age,	22
"Between 40 and 50 years of age,	4
"Between 50 and 60 years of age,	3
"Between 60 and 70 years of age,	1

"Beyond seventy, not one!

"What a lesson is this on the delay of conversion! How rapidly it cuts off the hope of delaying, as they continue on in life, making darker and darker the prospect as they are nearing the tomb! How rapidly the prospect of conversion diminishes! far more rapidly than the prospect of life! Let the sinner delay till he is twenty years old—he has lost more than half the probability of salvation he had at twelve! Let him delay till he is thirty years old, and he has lost three-fourths of the probability of salvation which he had at twenty. Let him delay till he has reached forty years, and only twenty-nine probabilities out of a thousand remain to him. Let him delay till he has reached fifty years, and beyond fifty there remains to him only fourteen out of a thousand! What a lesson upon delay! What an emphatic lesson!"

Oh, my young friend, run not the dreadful risk. Trifle not thus with the precious interests of the soul. Now is your accepted time, and your day of salvation. Seize upon the present auspicious moment. Yield to the drawings of divine love now—now, while the Spirit and the bride still cry, come.

My aged friend, let not those grey hairs be laid in the tomb under the weight of unrepented sin. Life with you is almost closed. You must be quick. Dark, dark indeed, are your prospects ; yet your case may not be utterly hopeless. Your probation is yet prolonged, and where sin has abounded there grace may yet much more abound.

CHAPTER XIII.

A DEATH-BED REPENTANCE.

SHOULD the procrastinating sinner be asked how long he intends to put off the duty of repentance, he would probably return a very indefinite and evasive answer. He would tell you that he has fixed upon no particular time. If the duty be attended to before the close of life, he cares not how far it is crowded into the unknown future. If not sooner, he calculates that he will certainly obtain mercy in his last hour. *A death-bed repentance* is the sandy foundation on which rest the hopes of thousands.

No delusion is more common, and yet none more ruinous. This is the fatal rock on which the souls of men are continually wrecked. Under this delusion, every present offer of salvation is neglected, in hope that the patience of God which has waited so long already, will continue to wait unto the end.

Will the delaying reader give me his attention while I propose to him a few questions, demanding a most candid and deliberate answer.

Upon what, let me ask, is your hope of salvation in the hour of death based?

Is it upon *any encouragement which you find in the sacred Scriptures?* Point me to the chapter or the verse where any such encouragement is afforded. Who can suppose that God has written a single word filled to inspire the hope that men may willfully spend their whole life in sin, and then secure his favor at the close?

I know that we have on record a remarkable instance of conversion in a dying hour; and it is in view of this solitary instance that multitudes flatter themselves that all will be well with them in the end. The case of the penitent thief, however, is so peculiar that it can furnish but little ground of hope to the procrastinating sinner. When the Saviour dies a second time upon the cross and another attestation of his divine power is required, then may you look for a similar interposition. Let it be remembered that this is *the only case* of the kind of which we have any record, on the sacred page. We read of the conversion of thousands; but only of *one* in his last moments—"one," as has justly been remarked, "that sinners may not despair; and only one that they may not presume." Suppose it had once happened that a person had leaped down from a lofty precipice without losing his life, would it be prudent for ten thousand other people to run the risk, and leap down after him?" As the subjects of divine grace were formerly selected, not from the dying, but from the living, so, we have reason to believe, will be the ordering of infinite wisdom in all future time.

Why do the Scriptures abound with such urgent calls to immediate repentance? Why do they announce to us in such emphatic terms—"Behold now is the accepted time; behold now is the day of salvation?" Why do they admonish us to "seek the Lord while he may be found; and call upon him while he is near?" if, after all, men may refuse salvation now, and yet obtain it at any time they may think proper. All the commands to repentance relate to the present moment, and all the promises of the gospel belong to a present repentance.

Upon what, then, does the reader base his hope of repentance and salvation in a dying hour—*upon the sentiments of good men?* Their unanimous testimony is that a death-bed repentance is a matter of most fearful uncertainty. Some have entertained the opinion that such a repentance is never genuine; all agree in regarding it as extremely hazardous. Nor need we wonder at this. There are circumstances that may well render such a repentance doubtful; and among these I may refer to the fact that in almost every instance where individuals, apparently at death's door, have recovered, the contrition which they may have manifested during their sickness, has passed away like the morning cloud and the early dew. What pastor could not tell of the disappointment he has experienced in such cases? After a pastorate of forty years, one remarks: "that he has not met with a single instance of sick-bed repentance turning out to be genuine." Another says: "In my not short ministerial life, I recollect but one man, who after making promises of fidelity in sickness, remembered to keep them after he got well."

"For years," says a distinguished divine, "I have watched the lives of those who recovered after experiencing what they considered a death-bed repentance, and out of *twenty* cases where we should have had no doubt of their happiness, had they died, but *one* single individual ever united with the church."

"A minister in England, settled over an

extensive parish, states, that of two thousand persons whose cases came under his notice, who, in anticipation of death, appeared truly penitent, only two of all who were again restored to health, afforded evidence of a saving change."

"A pious English physician once stated, that he had known some three hundred sick persons, who, expecting soon to die, had been led, as they supposed, to repentance for their sins, and saving faith in Christ, but had eventually been restored to health. Only ten of all this number, so far as he knew, gave any evidence of being really regenerated. Soon after their recovery, they plunged, as a general thing, into all the follies and vices of the world."

Let me state one instance among many. "A few years since, a pastor in one of the quiet villages of Massachusetts, was called to visit a sick man, who was supposed to be dying. The disease was violent; but reason was unimpaired, and his affrighted soul was trembling with a consciousness that he was not prepared to meet the Searcher of hearts. Eternity was opening before him: neglected warnings, misspent Sabbaths, a slighted Bible, admonitions scoffed at—in short, a life spent in sin shut out the light of hope from his heart, and his agony of spirit was almost past endurance.

"The physician pronounced his case alarming; but still it was not impossible that his life might be spared. When the pastor came into the room, the sufferer raised his eyes, fixed them upon him with eager earnestness, and then said, 'Mr. P——, before you pray for me, I wish you to put your hand on my heart, and make a solemn covenant with me, that if God spares my life, and I return to my sinful habits, you will come to me, and tell me just how I looked this morning, tell me what I said, and how I felt, when I thought myself so near the bar of God!' A group of weeping friends, the stillness of a sick room, the groans of the sufferer, seemed to forebode that death was already present to ratify the covenant made at that solemn hour.

"Mr. S—— slowly recovered, and in the course of a few months was again seated in the bar-room with scoffers, taking the name of God in vain; and with more than his wonted hardness of heart before his late warning, he defied the truth of God.

"True to his promise, the pastor called on him, met him alone at the house, and solemnly told him, as he had requested, how he looked, and what he said when he thought eternity was to reveal the secret motives of the heart. The scene was vividly placed before his mind, but his heart was like the ice-berg of the Northern seas. God permitted him to live many years, and when the fatal summons came, he entered on eternity, to all appearance, without a Saviour, without hope."

But let me press the inquiry still further, Upon what does the delaying sinner base his hope of salvation in his last moments? *Upon the mercy of God?* We cannot speak in too exalted terms of that mercy; but it is mercy exercised under the direction of Divine wisdom, and in perfect harmony with Divine justice. Rich and free as that mercy is, it has its limits, where it turns to vengeance. We know that it follows no sinner beyond the grave, and why may it not be brought to a close before the close of life?

The criminal presumption of those who deliberately postpone repentance to the last hours of probation, is such that we need not wonder if it should be visited with the tokens of Divine displeasure. Is it reasonable to suppose that after mercy has plead so long, and plead in vain, that it will continue to wait the sinner's time? "It is a people of no understanding;" says the Almighty; "therefore he that made them will not have mercy on them, and he that formed them will show them no favor."—Is. xxvii. 11. "Because I have called, and ye refused; I have stretched out my hand, and no man regarded; but ye have set at nought all my counsel and would none of my reproof: I also will laugh at your calamity; I will mock when your fear cometh."—Prov. i. 24—33.

A few years since, the writer preached to his people on the danger of delaying repentance to a death-bed. I stated that I had but little confidence in the genuineness of such a repentance, and solemnly warned my hearers to beware of thus hazarding the precious interests of the soul. I remarked, at the same time, that if any of them should be guilty of such presumption, I would do for them what I could, though at the last hour of life; that should I be sent for to visit them in their dying-chamber, I would respond to the call, even were they to send for me at midnight. Little did I suppose, when I delivered that sermon, that I should so soon have occasion to fulfill my promise.

During that week, at a late hour in the night, a carriage drove up to my door to convey me about three miles into the country, to visit a young man on the borders of eternity.

Never can I erase from my mind the scene that I witnessed when I entered the room. The youth had been ill for some months; but had, all the while, until this morning, entertained the hope of recovery. No sooner did he begin seriously to apprehend the approach of death, than he was seized with the most terrible remorse, and in the most plaintive strains, cried aloud for mercy.

When I inquired whether he had never felt any concern about his salvation before, he referred me to a conversation I had with him at the close of one of our evening services. "With your hand upon my shoulder," said he, "you invited me to come to Jesus; but I said, No—not now!" I expressed to him my deep regret that he had thus stifled his convictions, and then endeavored to point him to Christ as his sole dependence and hope. In the most affecting manner he lamented his folly, and continued his cry for mercy,—warning his weeping friends not to imitate his unhappy example. Before the morning's dawn his lips were sealed in death, and his spirit had passed into the presence of God. The rest we must leave to the revelations of the future.

> "Death, 'tis a melancholy day,
> To those who have no God;
> When the poor soul is forced away,
> To seek her last abode."

I ask again, Does *observation* afford any encouragement to hope that salvation may be secured in a dying hour? What are the facts in the case? Some of these have already been stated; but let us notice them a little more in detail.

Numbers die just as they live, utterly insensible to their condition as sinners, and without the least expression of concern as to their future destiny. The slumber of sin remains unbroken to the last. They die as die the beasts of the field, without hope, without fear. Never do they awake to a consciousness of their peril, until they awake in despair.

Others, indeed, are brought to *tremble in*

anticipation of their future prospects; but it is only to experience the premonition of their impending doom. They do not even attempt to pray for mercy; or, if they do, no answer of peace is returned to their agonized spirits. With a "certain fearful looking for of judgment, and fiery indignation," they enter upon their state of retribution, and receive their final sentence.

The *fears of others are followed by hope.* After a season of great mental conflict, they, at length, trust that they have obtained forgiveness, and calmly resign themselves to the stroke of death; and yet even in those cases that may appear to us the most hopeful, we have reason to "rejoice with trembling." How many instances of apparent conversion occur among persons in health, and in the full exercise of their mental powers, which, in the end, prove utterly spurious. If such cases occur under the most favorable circumstances, how little dependence can be placed on the exercises of a death-bed.

The dying sinner is particularly liable to self-deception. He feels that he is perishing, and like a drowning man, is ready to seize even a straw. Anxious to obtain some evidence that God has become reconciled to him, he is under a strong temptation to regard every change in his feelings as favorable, and thus to cry peace, when there is no peace. Let the idea once get possession of his mind that he is prepared to die, and the natural effect must be to allay his fears, and even fill him with joy. And yet all this may take place while he yet remains a stranger to the work of regeneration, and his hope may prove like "the giving up of the ghost."

What reason, then, has the delaying sinner to hope that he will obtain salvation in his dying moments? Will he then enjoy a *more favorable time, or be placed in more favorable circumstances?*

A more favorable time? *You may have no time at all.* Instead of weeks or months of confinement to a sick-chamber, you may be seized with sudden death, and with scarcely a moment's warning, find yourself in the presence of God. How many are continually dying in this manner—in apparent health one hour, the next in the cold embrace of death—one hour mingling with the scenes of earth, the next inhabitants of the world of spirits. "Because there is wrath,—beware, lest he take thee away with his stroke; then a great ransom cannot deliver thee."

But suppose, dear reader, you should be confined to your bed with protracted sickness, will you find such a season more favorable to repentance than the present? What! when the body is racked with pain; when the powers of the mind are enfeebled, and when reason is perhaps dethroned? Is *that* the favorable period to settle the great question respecting your eternal salvation, to secure a valid title to an inheritance in heaven? Who would leave an affair of such moment to the mercy of a few lingering, distracted hours? What is done under these circumstances, must necessarily be done in a hurry. But little time may be afforded for self-examination; and however protracted may be your sickness, you can have but little opportunity to test the reality of your conversion; and when you imagine that all is well, you may be under the influence of a most fatal self-delusion.

You hope to repent on a death-bed.—Why? Will your heart then be any more disposed to obey God than now? Will your present opposition to his claims suddenly give way to holy submission? Will the excuses you are accustomed to urge, be abandoned? Will your repugnance to be saved on the terms of the Gospel be, at once, followed by cordial acquiescence? Free as you may then be from worldly embarrassments, may not the same heart of enmity against God; the same love of sin—the same disrelish for holy exercises, that prevent you from becoming a Christian while you are in health, prevent you from becoming one on a bed of sickness and death?

If you are brought to repentance at all, it must be by the agency of the Holy Spirit; but are you sure that he will then continue his gracious influence? Be assured it is not sickness, not pain, not death that can subdue the rebellious heart of man. Neither these nor any other means will prove effectual without the operation of Divine grace; and that grace, refused now, may then be utterly withdrawn, leaving you to all the darkness and horror of eternal despair.

Oh, venture not your eternal all upon the baseless hope of a death-bed repentance. Plant not your dying pillow with thorns of regret. You have but one day of grace; put not off the work of salvation until the close of that day. Every moment is precious, and you know not but on the decision of the present may be suspended your weal or wo for eternity. It should be the business of man's whole life on earth to prepare for heaven.

CHAPTER XIV.

THE DECISION.

"HOW LONG," said the prophet to his undecided hearers, "*halt ye between two opinions?*" With the same expostulation we now meet the hesitating reader. It is to be hoped that you have, at least, been brought to the serious consideration of the things pertaining to your eternal peace. You are no longer that thoughtless being you once were. Religion begins to assume an aspect of importance which it never did before, and you are seriously revolving the question: "Shall I now devote myself to God, or, shall I continue to defer to the future his claims to my love and obedience?"

Now, this is a most painful state of mind—to say nothing of its exceeding guilt and folly.

A state of indecision, where any important interest is at stake, is always a source of uneasiness; how much more when it relates to the destiny of the soul. The *careless* sinner may enjoy a temporary peace. He sees not the slippery steep on which he stands, and the fiery billows that roll beneath; and hence, with heedless steps he rushes on to ruin. But it is different with the *awakened* sinner. Your spiritual slumber has been broken, the claims of God press heavily upon your conscience. Sin no longer appears to you as a trifle, but as a crime; visions of eternity haunt your mind; the world has lost its charms, and a voice from the eternal throne, admonishes you to flee from the coming wrath, and to lay hold on eternal life.

The mind, in this state, has reached a most solemn crisis. It will probably not remain thus long. A decision of some kind will be made, and made soon. There are two ways in which the reader may get rid of this painful suspense. He may yield to his convictions of truth and duty, and by faith in Jesus, have his agitated, troubled bosom set forever at rest; or, he may banish his present anxiety, and sink back into his former stupidity and unconcern.

Which will you do? What decision ought you to make? What decision will you ere long wish you had made?

A present decision is not only reasonable but practicable. There is no necessity for remaining in this state of hesitation a single moment. You cannot decide too promptly if only you decide aright. The transition from impenitence to penitence, from unbelief to faith, must, from the nature of the case, be instantaneous. Religion must have a beginning, and it begins only when the heart is surrendered to God, and embraces with a living faith his plan of redeeming mercy. And why may it not, why should it not begin *now?* When the mind is agitated with the question of duty, even a moment's delay may prove fatal. We are informed of a lady, who, when awakened to a sense of her lost condition as a sinner, resolved to repent before the close of the day. The Spirit of God was urging her to a *present* decision, but her purpose was to decide some time during the day. Night came on, but it found her still in her sins, and almost as unconcerned as she had been for months previously.

The next morning her religious impressions revived, and again the resolution was formed "to begin religion before the close of that day." With this the anxiety of her mind again subsided, and the day passed off, as did the preceding one, leaving her still unreconciled to God. On the third day her convictions returned. Again she renewed her resolution, and again was it violated as before. Thus she went on resolving and breaking her resolutions, until her anxiety vanished, and she relapsed into her former indifference.

About three months afterwards, she was laid upon a bed of death. Her sickness was short, of only five days' continuance. Her anguish now became intolerable. She felt that it was *too late—too late ;* and referring to the plausible resolution she had made to repent so soon, she called it "*the fatal resolution*," and she earnestly begged the minister who visited her, to charge all the youth in his congregation not to stifle their convictions by a mere resolution to repent, without carrying it into immediate effect.

How different this case from that of a young lady, who, on receiving intelligence of the sudden death of a pious young friend, after some moments of serious thought, exclaimed, "What a terrible thing it would be were I to be thus summoned away !" Another pause succeeded, and she added, "I will be a Christian!" Pondering a moment longer, she continued, "I will be one to-day !" This did not satisfy her troubled spirit, and she said with emphasis, "I will be one *now !*" The decision was fully made, and she retired to open her Bible, and cast herself in prayer upon its promises at the foot of Calvary.

Dear reader, shall not that determination now be yours? Will you not repent and believe now? All these promises in reference to the future, are evasive and perilous. Until we gain your present purpose to repent we gain nothing. The purpose to repent hereafter, involves, of course, the purpose to disobey God now; and every renewed act of disobedience, with whatever resolutions it may be accompanied, enhances both your guilt and danger.

Trusting that you have been brought to the decision to yield yourself at once to God, let me now say:—see that it is done *intelligently*. Count the cost. Weigh the matter well. Look not merely at the privileges, but also at the responsibilities and sacrifices of the Christian life. Study the sacred word. Let it be the man of your counsel, and the guide of your life. Raise your heart to God, and plead with him for the enlightening influence of his Spirit, to unfold to you the glorious scheme of redemption, and to lead you in "the way everlasting."

See, too, that your consecration to God be *unreserved.* Keep nothing back from him. He must have the whole heart or nothing. Be not satisfied with anything short of a thorough conversion, a radical change. Remember, that what is demanded is not mere resolutions and promises, but the actual surrender of yourself to God, body and soul—all you are and all you have forever—not a little seriousness, not a partial reformation, not a mere attention to the externals of religion, but a new birth, a new creation. Dig deep, and lay the foundation low. Build not on the sand, but on the rock. "Other foundation can no man lay than that is laid, which is Jesus Christ."

Let your dedication to God be a *permanent* one—not for a season, but for life—for time and eternity. Join yourself to him in a *perpetual* covenant, never to be revoked. Put not your hand to the plough, and then look back. Begin not in the Spirit, and end in the flesh. Only "he that endureth to the end, shall be saved."

And having thus given yourself to God in *private*, embrace the first opportunity to dedicate yourself to him in *public*. "With the heart man believeth unto righteousness, and with the mouth confession is made unto salvation." Come out from the world—identify yourself with the people of God—pledge yourself in the presence of the Searcher of hearts, before the church, and the world, that henceforth it is your fixed purpose to live not for yourself, but for him who ransomed you with his blood. This is both your privilege and your duty. You owe it to Christ, you owe it to the church, you owe it to yourself thus openly to espouse the cause of truth, and enroll yourself among the followers of the Lamb. You thus obey your Saviour's dying command, seal your vow of allegiance around the sacred board, place yourself under the watch and care of the church, and unite your prayers and energies with the friends of Zion, in urging forward the triumphs of redeeming grace. Go, then, trusting to an almighty arm for support, and offer yourself up publicly on the altar of God, to be his willing servant forever; and as you seal the unalterable contract, call upon God, angels, and men to witness the sincerity of your engagement.

> "Here in thy courts I leave my vow,
>   And thy rich grace record;
> Witness, ye saints, who hear me now,
>   If I forsake the Lord."

Having taken the oath of allegiance to the King of Zion, see that you prove faithful to his cause. Never betray that cause either by open inconsistency, or by cold indifference, either from the influence of fear or shame. Never let your tongue falter in pronouncing the "name which is above every name." Learn to glory in the cross. Strive to win others to Christ. Invite all to whom you can gain access, to accompany you in your march.

Look upon the world in the light of a Saviour's cross, the light of eternity. Begin and carry forward all your efforts to do good with prayer. Cultivate the spirit of expansive benevolence, and let your whole deportment evince the sincerity of your profession, and convince the world that you have been with Jesus.

Here the writer and reader must part, not, we trust, without the hope of meeting eventually in that world of bliss where our redemption shall be completed, and where, with united voice, we shall join in the triumphant song: "UNTO HIM THAT LOVED US, AND WASHED US FROM OUR SINS IN HIS OWN BLOOD, AND HATH MADE US KINGS AND PRIESTS UNTO GOD AND HIS FATHER: TO HIM BE GLORY AND DOMINION FOREVER AND EVER. AMEN."

THE END.

www.ingramcontent.com/pod-product-compliance
Lightning Source LLC
LaVergne TN
LVHW021357110826
845150LV00007B/1683

* 9 7 8 1 4 2 5 5 1 4 1 9 8 *